Praise for *The Prepared*

T0023461

"At a time when integrating career
affairs is more critical than ever for meeting American higher
education's historic mission of educating for democracy,
this book offers compelling practical advice for connecting
curriculum to career through high-impact practices."

> **—LYNN PASQUERELLA**, president of the Association of
> American Colleges & Universities (AAC&U)

"This book is so real and honest! I wish I had this when I
first started out in my career. What Kyyah is doing with this
book is so vital to the career growth and survival of every
human being... Every parent should read this book and then
gift it to their child! "

> **—NANCY BARROWS**, MS CC-SLP, LAUSD educator &
> speech language pathologist

"The information and steps in this book are shared through
relatable and authentic stories, ensuring less career angst
among college students."

> **—BRIAN SCHULMAN**, CEO of Voice Your Vibe

"Hungry to learn? Ambitious? Curious? High-achieving, or
just want the answers on how to navigate the beginning of
your future? *The Prepared Graduate* is the insightful read
you need."

> **—CAROLINE STOKES**, author of *Elephants Before Unicorns*
> and founder of FORWARD

Real Clients, Real Results

"Looking for a job at the height of the pandemic was extremely challenging, but one résumé session with Career Savage [Kyyah] got me several follow-up calls. I now work in tech!"
    —JADA, 21

"I am thankful for everything Kyyah did for my girls! She did a splendid job guiding them through their college application process. They said she really challenged them, and that they feel like better writers as a result. That's pretty cool."
    —ALLISON, mother of two seniors in high school

"After booking a career consult with Kyyah, I felt much more confident about pursuing my career path. Kyyah is an excellent resource for career advice. She understands the importance of networking and working with recruiters and hiring managers. I would recommend anyone who feels uncertain about their career trajectory to book a consultation."
    —EVAN, 25

"As a working professional navigating career positions, consulting with Career Savage [Kyyah] was key in facilitating job negotiations. Her experience and knowledge gave me insight to streamline my decision-making process."
    —ZUSI, 33

"The Career Savage [YouTube] videos helped me discover my true passion in life and to be confident in everything I do! I love the way Kyyah carries herself and the advice she gives to help me become a better version of myself!"

—NNEKA, 23

"Career Savage [Kyyah] is like an angel sent from heaven to help people like me. I started watching her YouTube videos a while ago and believe it or not she helped me a lot as far as my career is concerned. Right now, I am working on my bachelor's degree and thanks to her insight and guidance I feel prepared for the future. Career Savage made me fall in love with my field and for that I am beyond thankful!"

—FRANK, 22

"When in doubt, press those dial buttons! Who knew the effect one phone call with Career Savage [Kyyah] would have? Our conversation brought everything into perspective and has given me hope for a brighter future in my industry. Kyyah's advice and insight was all I needed! She was so willing to help and forthcoming with answers and suggestions I didn't know I needed. Career Savage came through for me."

—B, 35

"The person who interviewed me said I had a really nice résumé. Career Savage [Kyyah] held it down!"

—JAY, 21

"I came across Career Savage [Kyyah] on YouTube while I was contemplating which degree I wanted to pursue in graduate school. I was deciding between two healthcare master's and didn't know which one to choose. All I knew was that I wanted to study something that would not only help me make a difference in my community but also satisfy my inquisitive nature. After watching a few videos, I then came across one that discussed a completely different healthcare career option. One I knew nothing about! The way she described this newly discovered field made me want to learn more about it. I felt like I had finally found a career that would make me happy! I have since taken the step in applying for a graduate program in clinical management with a concentration in regulatory science. The thing I love most about Career Savage [Kyyah] is that she doesn't settle, and she doesn't worry about changing her mind or pursuing other passions all while building her STEM career. She lets you know that it's okay to change your mind, to go after your dreams, and to accept whatever happens. She once said she didn't know if she would go to medical school or become vice president of a pharmaceutical company. She said she would just let the cards fall where they may. As someone who consistently stresses about the future, those words were so comforting to me. It let me know that I can do so many things and that I don't have to stay in just one place or focus on one project for the rest of my life! I am now excited about going back to school and dedicating some time to other passions and projects. Thank you [Kyyah] for everything that you do! Your words helped me more than you'll ever know!"

—PAOLA, 32

"I have so much to say…but what I will say is I am just glad to have stumbled upon the Career Savage YouTube channel. After watching Kyyah's videos I am on my way to pursuing a career in health and exploring the amazing versatility the field brings! I feel that I'm unlimited in possibilities and that I can decide to work wherever my heart resides."

—VICK, 19

"A lot of people give career advice but Career Savage [Kyyah] gives *honest* and realistic advice! She taught me that it's okay not to pursue medical school and that was a difficult thing for me to let go of. Thanks to her YouTube videos I learned what I really want to do with my life. I hope Kyyah keeps educating, advising, and empowering people because we all need someone like her when navigating our careers!"

—GRACE, 20

"After graduating from college in May 2021, I was sure the only next step for me was to pursue a career in medicine. I was a pre-health biology major throughout college and was never told there were other paths I could explore outside of medical school. I was always told that my options were to become a doctor or teach high school biology. Stumbling across Career Savage was *the* biggest blessing! I now know I have options outside of going to medical school. Since discovering Career Savage I have begun networking with the right people to ensure I am placed in a position that best suits my talents and interests!"

—ZAKAU, 21

THE
PREPARED
GRADUATE

THE PREPARED GRADUATE

Find Your Dream Job, Live the Life You Want, Step Into Your Purpose

KYYAH ABDUL

mango
PUBLISHING

CORAL GABLES

For permission requests, please contact the publisher at:
Mango Publishing Group
2850 S Douglas Road, 4th Floor
Coral Gables, FL 33134 USA
info@mango.bz

For special orders, quantity sales, course adoptions and corporate sales, please email the publisher at sales@mango.bz. For trade and wholesale sales, please contact Ingram Publisher Services at customer.service@ingramcontent.com or +1.800.509.4887.

The Prepared Graduate: Find Your Dream Job, Live the Life You Want, and Step Into Your Purpose

Library of Congress Cataloging-in-Publication number: 2021945307
ISBN: (print) 978-1-64250-756-0, (ebook) 978-1-64250-757-7
BISAC category code BUS037020, BUSINESS & ECONOMICS / Careers / Job Hunting

In honor of my little sister, Zafirah.
You were destined for greatness.

Contents

Introduction

"Luck is preparation meeting opportunity."

—OPRAH WINFREY

My biology 1 professor said to me, "I don't think you'll be able to keep up with the class. You may want to take a semester off school."

As a first-semester freshman, I managed to get strep throat persistently. It resulted in extreme fatigue and a lack of appetite. Rather than provide solutions that would keep me on track for graduation, my professor proposed I withdraw from their class that semester. As you read through this guide, you will learn I don't take direction from others well and this is the first example. I completed all my assignments on time and requested lecture notes from my peers, reading them while in and out of my lethargy. I completed my freshman year *without* withdrawing and graduated from college on time.

"You'd be better off applying to community college," my high school guidance counselor said.

The standard of excellence at my high school meant having at least a 3.7 GPA. Because my average fell slightly below the standard, my counselor felt I wasn't four-year-college material. While I encourage people to take the community college route to save money and figure out what they may want to do in life, I proudly applied to and successfully attended a four-year university.

The Career Advice Others Give

Be it subconsciously or consciously, it's always been funny to me how people in positions of guidance sometimes manage to try to steer you further away from achieving your goals. They introduce doubt, which sometimes results in your questioning your capabilities. Living through these instances, I have learned that no one can tell you how to live your life, and, more importantly, no one should tell you *exactly* how to navigate your career. There are great differences between poor guidance, no guidance, and career control. My high school guidance counselor and biology 1 professor offered poor guidance, whereas my immigrant parents attempted to control my career. We will touch more on this later. As for not having guidance, well, you will learn how I associate career centers with that inaction. No matter who is around us, offering us advice or guiding us through uncharted territory, we must remain cognizant of what *we* want for *ourselves*.

Each person was created to live their life, fulfilling their unique intended purpose. If any generations understand this concept, it's Millennials and Generation Z. We understand our careers are merely one aspect of life and refuse to become cogs in a machine or work for companies that cannot respect our needs for innovation and desires for individuality. Approximately two million people graduate from college and earn their bachelor's degree each year.[1] Some enter the workforce, pursuing passions related to their major, and others return home to their parents lost and confused because though they have a degree, no one has opted to hire them. Some manage to swing a job at their parents' place of employment, and some use their pricey degree to work as a cashier at Lululemon. It's a phenomenon that's left me puzzled since graduating from college. I used to wonder why so many people struggle to find jobs related to their major post-college. It feels as if the answer is so simple, yet the problem persists. The issue is a lack of experience in addition to insufficient career guidance. Sure, there are career centers on each college campus, but what do they *actually* do, and who is running the place? Are there industry experts advising students? Do they understand the current job market? At my alma mater, the career center was known to the students as the fraternity and sorority hangout. I was always socializing nearby, but seldom was I there for career-related matters. The one time I did go, I left feeling disappointed. I don't recall ever receiving any *real* advice from anyone in that building. Then there is your assigned college advisor. The one who has thousands of other students to advise in addition to a full teaching schedule. It always seems impossible to land a meeting with them and when you do get the chance to speak, the focus is on the classes you should take the upcoming semester. If the career center can't help and advisors are too busy, who should advise students on what to do after graduation?

As a younger millennial born on the cusp of Generation Z, I consider myself a Zillennial. So, on behalf of both generations, I want to address baby boomers and Generation X. Millennials and Generation Z do not want their hands held. We *actually* are not lazy, despite current misconceptions. While we do not want to be coddled, we *do* want relevant career advice. We *do* want help with our LinkedIn profiles, cover letters, and résumés. We *do* want to know what a recruiter is and how to get in touch with one. We *do* want suggestions on where to work part-time while in school, and we don't mean that typical work-study option where our day-to-day consists of signing people into the library.

Beyond the Millennial and Generation Z cohorts, college students to come will likely desire the same.

I hear the outcry of young people. This is why, in this guide, I will share with you my knowledge and experience to ensure you graduate with a job in your field. After you read *The Prepared Graduate*, you'll feel prepared to effectively navigate corporate America, your career, and post-graduation life. There's no contingency plan! All you must do is follow my advice. I want nothing more than to get you one step closer to living a fulfilling life and using that degree you took out so many student loans for. Everything college students need to achieve success after college is addressed in this book.

Growing up, my traditional Nigerian mother would reiterate that her children should begin to work whenever legally possible. She didn't care what the job was so long as we were getting experience in whatever piqued our interests. For example, if I wanted to become a police officer, she would have told me to intern at a precinct or become an assistant for a criminal defense attorney. Since I loved medicine and science, she always encouraged me to gain medical and scientific experience. Some will say it's typical of a Nigerian American girl to pursue science, but as you read through the stories I share, you will understand that my medical pursuit was not traditional. This is important to keep in mind: your journey will look different compared to those of your peers. My journey isn't *exactly* what your journey will look like. For this reason, disregard the steps your friends are taking and focus solely on your own career journey. As I focused on my career path, the one thing I never forgot was my mother's advice on gaining professional work experience.

During my sophomore year of college, I decided it was time to get a job. I refused to work anywhere that veered from my professional development. My mother's advice kept me on track in terms of working in places that would leave me better off come graduation day. My goal was clear: *get any job related to science and/or medicine.* I walked into a few CVS pharmacies telling anyone who would listen, "I would like to work in the pharmacy."

Many of the technicians and pharmacists would blankly stare at me and say, "Go apply online."

I opted not to apply online because I felt my application would get lost in the shuffle. Walking into every CVS within a fifteen-mile radius resulted in my getting a job as a licensed pharmacy technician at a newly built location three miles away from my university. CVS paid for my three-month technician training and my state pharmacy technician license. I dedicated two days to my search, and just like that, I got the job! This is the first and most crucial key to setting yourself up for a smooth transition into life after graduation. *Put your education into practice sooner rather than later.* You may be thinking, "I am a senior; it's already too late." The keywords here are "sooner rather than later." You still have time.

The Birth of Career Savage

Gaining professional work experience related to my major was the only career advice I ever took from my mother. From sophomore year of college on, I decided I would follow my own career advice. I would consider outside advice but only act on the guidance I thought served my best interests. If I listened to everyone's advice regarding my career, I would probably be riddled with anxiety, scrolling through TikTok all day, confused about who to listen to and what to do with my life.

I did my own research and, based on my findings, made appropriate decisions for *my life*. I mapped out multiple three-month plans and a three-year plan. I had three-month plans for each semester of my junior and senior years and a three-year plan for my post-graduation years. Of course, my yearly plans were fine-tuned the more experience I gained, but I intended to have a foundation for the direction I wanted to move in. I researched career advice for Millennials and Generation Z in my spare time and spoke with an array of people in my network. I spent hours on the phone with job recruiters while scrolling through LinkedIn, engaging with my connections and making more connections. The more I researched and learned, the more prepared I felt.

While formulating my career plans, I wanted to test my decreasing faith in career centers, and so one day, I went in for advice. I submitted my résumé for review, and when it was returned weeks later, the comments were irrelevant. Nonetheless, I made the requested changes and took my résumé to the hiring manager at the CVS I worked for. I wanted the opinion of an *actual* employer. Everything I was instructed to remove from my résumé, he inquired about. He was also displeased with the overall aesthetic of my résumé. The career center had told me that the appearance of this important document did not matter. Today, we know that aesthetics, even in the most mundane career fields, always matter. Your résumé doesn't need to have your photo and fancy illustrations to be considered aesthetically pleasing. Your résumé simply needs to be clean and concise. I only went *once* for career advice and instead opted for summer cookouts held outside the building because the novice "career advisors" I engaged with were giving me information completely left field of what career professionals in my field were saying.

As a result of my test, I stopped listening to individuals giving outdated career advice, and that's how Career Savage was born.

What Is a Career Savage?

A Career Savage is the ultimate beast in their career. They know how to navigate through their profession/career field in such a way that their advancements can't go unnoticed. You can be a Career Savage at any age and in any area, so long as you do everything necessary to maximize your potential and conquer your *why*. As a college senior, you may not have defined your *why* just yet, and that is okay. Sometimes your *why* is uncovered while gaining your professional experiences. You can still be a Career Savage as a senior in college. Your full-time occupation right now is student, and as a student reading this guide, you will learn how to beast your way through senior year, placing you in a better position than most. I created Career Savage to help Millennials, Generation Z, and college students to become beasts at whatever they choose to do. We are expected to excel, but how do we accomplish this if we lack the proper information and tools?

Our generations are innovative, and I expect nothing less from future generations. Many of you reading this may even be interested in starting your own business. Throughout this book, you will also learn tips and tricks on how to navigate entrepreneurship. What you should know immediately is you don't need a business plan to start a business. That is, unless you are seeking investors or financial backing from a financial institution. If you want to focus on starting a business while conquering your professional career, you will also gain insightful instruction on how to pioneer such ambitions.

I'll share with you all the ways I gained career experience before graduating and used it to my advantage. This guide will give you the information you need to land a job utilizing your hard-earned degree. *The Prepared Graduate* is all about delivering accurate and relevant career advice to combat the increasing number of jobless graduates and graduates working jobs irrelevant to their career field.

What Are Your Career Plans?

I want you to stop and write in your planner, a notebook, or even here in this guide, what *you* think you want to do after graduation and why. As you consider what you want to accomplish, think of bigger goals that require you to achieve multiple steps before reaching the goal.

What do you want to do after graduation?
1)	Why?
2)	Why?
3)	Why?
4)	Why?
5)	Why?

If you could not find a reason as to *why* you want to pursue any of the avenues you have written down, chances are you don't want to pursue it. You likely think it's what you are supposed to do or what you need to do to be successful. Goals that lack vision or passion likely won't come to fruition.

Here's the list I wrote my senior year:

What I want to do after graduation:	
1) Further my education within the medical profession	*Why?* I have so many questions I can't seem to find the answer to. Researching sickle cell and malaria in Research Methods solidified my interest in pursuing medicine in some form. It's odd to me that sickle cell disease is so common, yet it's not as talked about as frequently as other diseases. Is it because it is a minority disease? Why is there such an insufficient amount of minority representation in healthcare? Many marginalized patients are being treated by people they can't relate to and diseases that disproportionately affect diverse populations are also researched by nondiverse populations. How can minorities reach their maximum quality of life with such a reality? Moreover, people of color are often stereotyped and misdiagnosed because of a nondiverse healthcare system. How can you treat people you don't fully understand? Whether I treat sickle cell patients or not, I know I want to transform how clinical research operates and address how America disregards the needs of minorities in general. On the macro level, science and medicine make sense to me. It's something I am effortlessly passionate about.

~~2) I want to become a realtor~~	~~Why? This is a pretty good side job. If I sell a couple of houses, I will be able to pay of my student loans.~~
~~3) I want to work in lab~~	~~Why? I think this will give me good clinical exposure.~~
4) I want to work for a pharmaceutical company	*Why?* I know I do not want to be a pharmacist. Working at CVS helped me figure that out. I am not sure how they [pharmacists] do it. What I do enjoy is the research side of pharmaceuticals. I read a lot about "Big Pharma" and think it would give me a unique perspective on contributing to the healthcare system without becoming a medical doctor.
5) I just want to use my degree and go from there	*Why?* I spent four years working toward my degree, and I'll be disappointed if I remain a pharmacy technician longer than anticipated.

Numbers two and three never came to fruition. I did not become a realtor, nor did I work in a lab. Working for realtors in high school painted a vivid image of wealth in my mind. I envisioned selling million-dollar homes in Los Angeles and popping bottles of Veuve at the end of every closing. In all honesty, I dislike real estate work. Sometimes you spend months looking for a home for buyers who may never make it to a closing date. Or worse, you spend months preparing to close with your transaction coordinator in hand, only for your buyers or sellers to back out. Then you're left with no commission and a new mission to find someone looking to seriously engage within the housing market. On top of that, you are responsible for deducting IRS tax fees, which can be tricky if you're not careful. Most importantly, if you are not a local socialite, it takes years to create a name for yourself and build up your book of business. I only wanted to pursue that venture for the money, and for that reason, I never completed my courses or took the exam to get my California real estate license. From the end of high school until now, my online real estate classes have been reactivated and deactivated more times than I can count.

I never worked in a lab because I never enjoyed laboratory work. The idea of running ELISA tests all day in isolation would have driven me off the deep end. When I would search for jobs post-graduation, I would receive leads on lab jobs and reroute them to my junk mail. Per my college advisor's guidance, I wanted to work in a lab to strengthen my résumé for medical school applications but never saw the advice through. I was not willing to be miserable for the possibility of looking like a good candidate. There are a million ways to get into medical school or any graduate program, and working in a lab is not the only way to do so. As you read through this book, you will learn how important it is to understand your *why*. You will not wholeheartedly pursue or complete anything if you cannot explain, with good reason, why you want to do it.

During your senior year, you are likely overburdened with classes and graduation-related tasks. That, or you have senioritis and are skipping the classes Sallie Mae is paying for. During this year, it is easy to feel overwhelmed just trying to figure out what to do post-graduation. Some of you may be interested in continuing your education. Others may be more interested in working immediately after graduating. There is a lot of anxiety associated with making all these decisions in what feels like so little time. Especially when you are making decisions for your future with minimal guidance. The majority of college seniors stress out about their future; I know I did. Here is the thing: if you take the initiative to apply for jobs, apply to graduate school, or even plan to backpack through northern Italy, it *will* happen for you. With the help of Career Savage, the success of your plans is inevitable.

PART I

FORGE FORWARD

CHAPTER 1

The Intensifying Struggle

"If there is no struggle, there is no progress."
—FREDERICK DOUGLASS

Eighty years ago, a college degree was seen as nothing more than a nice educational accessory for upper-class members of society.[2] It wasn't necessary for career advancement, nor was it necessary for obtaining wealth. However, things are different in the twenty-first century. College is no longer just a *nice to have*; it has become a *need to have*. And even when you have it, most people feel the path to secure career-related employment is still an uphill battle. Unfortunately, employers have the upper hand in demanding what they require of their employees to work for their organization and we, college students and graduates, are having a difficult time adjusting to such demands. For one, they require an abundance of experience or simply try to pay you next to nothing, despite your having an $80,000 degree. Many of us are stuck between: (1) what's the point of college if you graduate with so much debt, and (2) why don't I just start my own business instead of going to college?

According to the Bureau of Labor Statistics (BLS), 20 percent of new businesses fail within the first two years, 45 percent during the first five, and 65 percent during the first ten years.[3] Twenty-five percent of new businesses manage to make it past fifteen years,[3] and during that time, you can bet there were obstacles. The debt you acquire as a college student can equate to the same debt some businesses experience. No matter which path you embark on, it will be accompanied by its own set of stressors and difficulties. Deciding which path to take as an eighteen-year-old high school graduate is difficult. Often, students who decide not to go to college straight out of high school rarely go back to complete all four years. As students spend time deciding which struggle makes the most sense, unanswered questions begin to fill their heads.

What's the Purpose of College?

The purpose of college has changed over the years. Today, college feels like a culmination of historical purposes. Harvard University was the first college to be founded in the United States in 1636.[4] When Harvard first opened its doors, its main purpose was to train clergymen.[5] As more colleges began to follow in Harvard's footsteps, the pool of college students transitioned from clergymen to include America's elite.[2] Considering inflation, college wasn't nearly as expensive then as it is now, so why couldn't everyday Americans better their lives by getting a college degree? Middle to poor working-class families simply couldn't afford to trade a labor salary for an education. For over 180 years, the college system continued to signify prestige and remained true to its purpose of helping churches until 1819.

The University of Virginia was founded in 1819 by former US President Thomas Jefferson.[6] He was determined to make college more affordable and applicable to the public.[6] Rather than restricting college to aspiring clergymen, Jefferson aspired to have a public institution that would encourage average Americans to build upon their general knowledge. Jefferson's founding efforts at the University of Virginia kickstarted the public college education system. Similar to modern times, the government managed to have its hands in collegiate education. In 1862, Vermont Congressman Justin Morrill proposed the Morrill Land Grant Act, which would donate public land to selected states and territories to build colleges.[7] The colleges were expected to promote agricultural and mechanical arts, thus ensuring a plentiful educated workforce within these specific fields. So far, from 1636 through the 1860s, we can acknowledge the purpose of college shifting from solely an education rooted in religion to an education in practical knowledge.

In the early 1900s, another shift took place. Many people still did not feel college was necessary, so colleges and universities took a different approach to drive up enrollment. College soon became about *the experience*. The emphasis on many of our experiences in college—Greek life, parties, sports, and the overall appeal of how a campus looks—ramped up in the 1900s. Why do you think campus tours have become so instrumental in student's commitment decisions? It is not by coincidence; it's by design. While students should never base their college attendance decisions on turf football fields and keg parties, some students opt to attend colleges and universities with strong athletic teams, a great reputation, and engaging social events.

After the *experience* shift, came the shift to *requirement* from 1950 to 1970. President Franklin D. Roosevelt signed the Servicemen's Readjustment Act—better known as the GI Bill—into law on June 22, 1944,[8] and from then, the perception of college slowly began to change. The GI Bill was meant to provide tuition and living stipends for college or vocational programs, among other benefits, to veterans of World War II.[8] As a result of this aid, colleges and universities saw a noticeable increase in enrollment and bachelor's degrees awarded in the following years. According to the National Center for Education Statistics, approximately 432,000 bachelor's degrees were awarded in 1950,[9] six years after the GI Bill went into effect. The 1950s were truly the beginning of college attendance becoming the norm. Twenty years later, in 1970, 792,316 bachelor's degrees were awarded.[9] That's an 83 percent increase!

So what is the purpose of going to college in modern society? The purpose of attending college in the twenty-first century has become a mixture of all its original purposes. Students attend for the prestige, attainable knowledge, college experience, and the desire to meet career requirements.

The Prestige

Except for Cornell University and their class of 2024 (10.7 percent),[10] most Ivy League institutions have an overall acceptance rate well below 9 percent.[11] For the graduating class of 2025, Harvard University had an overall acceptance rate of 3.4 percent.[11] This small percentage is the result of Harvard's attempts to maintain its exclusivity. Ivy Leagues are deemed elite, and for this reason, a mass number of students strive to gain acceptance. If these students attended a non–Ivy League university or even a tier-three university, the chances of their success moving in a negative direction because they attended a school of less prestige is slim. Where you go to college, from a quality of education perspective, is likely no different from Stanford than it is at the University of New Haven. Look at the University of Southern California (USC), a top-tier private university. The overall acceptance rate for the class of 2025 was 12 percent.[12] Students and parents go to extreme lengths to gain acceptance into USC for no reason other than the prestige it holds. If you want to know how desperate people are to gain acceptance into schools such as USC and Stanford, take a deep dive into Operation Varsity Blues of 2019. In addition to some schools holding a certain prestige, college is generally a commodity inaccessible to all. For this reason, attending a four-year university or college, in itself, is distinguishable. Overall, prestige is undoubtedly a reason students choose to attend college.

Attainable Knowledge

YouTube, TikTok, and Instagram can teach you many things, but they can't teach you everything. Certain industries require you to obtain knowledge through traditional education before entering the workforce. Students interested in healthcare, law, engineering, and other technical fields can't rely on self-education for advancement. No one, and I mean *no one*, is interested in seeing people in crucial roles such as nursing with an education earned from social media. As our society evolves, maybe this is where higher education ends up, but until then, attained knowledge via a university degree is something many students desire and need to enter their fields of interest.

College Experience

The college experience grants you a certain freedom you've never experienced before. Many students transition from living with their parents to living an independent lifestyle. Beyond the unforgettable parties and historic athletic games, college is where many students discover who they are and who they aspire to be. Lifelong friendships and marriages are often birthed on the grounds of college campuses. Students gain more than an education—they gain a unique set of skills one can only obtain while pursuing a college education.

Career Requirements

The Georgetown Public Policy Institute stated that in 2020, 65 percent of jobs in the economy would require candidates to have a postsecondary education.[13] In 1973, of the 91 million jobs available, 9 percent of working people had a bachelor's degree while the majority, 40 percent, only held a high school diploma.[13] As we moved toward the twenty-first century, the number of high school diplomas in the workforce (as the terminal degree) began to shrink while the number of bachelor's degrees rose because of employers shifting job requirements. Many employers are fixated on college degrees because they believe the overall college experience produces a well-rounded individual capable of working and excelling in a professional environment.[14] As the population becomes more educated, employers are replacing non-college-educated retiring baby boomers with college-educated Millennials and Gen Z'ers. Whether we like the shift or not, it's becoming a career requirement to have a college degree for most jobs. Once artificial intelligence fully emerges, and more Americans become educated, it will only be a matter of time before the remaining jobs eventually require a college degree or no human interaction at all.

Do You Need College to Find a Good Job?

The definition of a good job is subjective. Some people feel a six-figure salaried job with benefits is phenomenal. Others feel a job offering a livable wage is amazing. Some may even feel any job that makes them happy regardless of the benefits and pay is a job worth committing to. As of 2019, the median living wage across the United States was $67,690 a year.[15] This salary aligns with the household income of those with some college ($61,911) and an associate degree ($69,573).[16] If you aspire to make $100,000 or more with one job, the likelihood of doing so without a college degree is less likely. Of course, freelancing is another avenue; it just may take longer. The median household income by educational attainment for a bachelor's degree in 2019 was $100,164 per year compared to $48,708 per year for high school graduates.[16] Therefore, you do need some form of college education if you consider a $60,000 or more salaried job good. This further supports the shift in the purpose of a college education. It's becoming more of a requirement not just for career advancement but also for survival.

2019 Median Household Income by Educational Attainment[16]	
High School Graduate (includes equivalency)	$48,708
Some College, No Degree	$61,911
Associate Degree	$69,573
Bachelor's Degree	$100,164
Master's Degree	$117,439
Professional Degree	$162,127
Doctorate	$142,347

Household Income in the US in 2019[17]	
Under $15,000	9.1%
$15,000 to $24,999	8%
$25,000 to $34,999	8.3%
$35,000 to $49,999	11.7%
$50,000 to $74,999	16.5%
$75,000 to $99,999	12.3%
$100,000 to $149,999	15.5%
$150,000 to $199,999	8.3%
$200,000 and over	10.3%

Many would like to believe college isn't necessary for success, wealth building, or career advancement, but more data each year continues to support the opposite. Additionally, many social factors affect a person's advancement. Telling a person from a marginalized group that college *isn't necessary* for their success doesn't consider their disadvantages in society. One race may come from a place of privilege, esteemed networks, generational wealth, and several other advantages to fall back on, should they opt to forgo a college education, whereas another race may not have such a privilege. Ultimately, needing college to secure a *good job* is at the discretion of prospective students. However, statistics continue to support the mutual exclusivity of college and success for many.

Why Graduates Struggle to Find a Job

Some struggles are ones we cannot help but experience, and as a result, we learn, grow, and build upon our resilience. Throughout the twenty-first century, educational advancement among college students has steadily increased. In 2011, 1.72 million graduates earned bachelor's degrees in the United States, compared to 1.99 million students in 2021.[1] While the number of graduates is increasing, that doesn't mean everyone graduating is securing a job in their field. Many people wonder why that is. If employers require a more educated staff and students are graduating with the education required, what is still preventing new graduates from receiving jobs after college?

Competition

As the candidate pool has become more educated and qualified over the past few decades, having a 4.0 GPA isn't enough to impress employers anymore. Some students are now graduating into the candidacy pool with years of volunteer, internship, and work experience, while a larger number graduate with only a degree. As the competition becomes stiffer, students need to work harder to set themselves apart to ensure they are offered a job in their field upon graduating. The key to setting yourself apart from the competition is to gain experiences while also gaining an education. As a senior in college, starting the journey of gaining work experience can feel challenging, but it's never too late. Achieving this goal is exactly what you'll learn as you read on.

No Experience

A classroom setting will always be based on theory. With work experience, you can put theoretical concepts to practice, which encourages employers to hire new graduates. As someone with professional work experience, you understand how to complete work in an office setting. You also pick up soft skills such as leadership, problem-solving, teamwork, communication, adaptability, and interpersonal skills. If you think working in group projects is enough to prepare you for an office setting, you've been misled. No group project will equip you with the necessary skills to navigate corporate America.

You may think any work experience applies to being considered a competitive applicant in the entry-level job pool, but as more people earn bachelor's degrees, students need to become more strategic. If you work part-time during the school year, it's not enough to be a cashier for a retailer when you are a pre-dentistry major. If you are working as a cashier to support yourself, continue to do so, but you should also complete a pre-dentistry volunteer experience or an internship for exposure in your field. Employers feel there is less of a gamble when entry-level employees come in with some sort of professional work experience, especially when it's related to the field.

Poor Networking

Current generations and those to come are born into a digital age, limiting their social interaction. The increased use of phones, laptops, and other technology has decreased their levels of human contact. Such contact is necessary for developing networking skills. A lack of networking abilities makes it that much harder for graduating students to secure employment in their fields of study. Blindly applying to hundreds of jobs is one way to find employment, but navigating a strong network is an easier way to secure an opportunity. With poor networks, students will only continue to struggle to find jobs out of college.

The Economy

Searching for a job is a difficult process with many layers. From competition to navigating networks, students have a lot to consider. One added layer students fail to think about is the state of the economy. People presume the economy solely affects workers and employers, but it truly hits college graduates even harder. Graduating into a volatile economy can force students to accept job offers unrelated to their field, ultimately delaying their career advancement. As a result, graduates earning potentials are set back by ten to fifteen years, equating to a $60,000 to $100,000 loss in lifetime earnings.[18] The Great Recession of 2008 left nearly nine million Americans unemployed while the US employment rate peaked at 10 percent.[19, 20] Businesses closed, halted hiring, and laid off staff to cut costs as students were graduating and looking for work to begin their careers. Many of the recession graduates of 2008 are still paying the price for their untimely matriculation. During the COVID-19 pandemic, unemployment peaked at a remarkable 14.8 percent in April 2020, just months before the class of 2020 graduated.[21] Many students who received job offers received follow-up emails rescinding those offers because of businesses struggling to generate income. The economy was in shambles throughout the COVID-19 recession, and many graduates opted to take jobs unrelated to their field to simply get by. This decision is common for graduates who receive their degrees in unstable times. Dissimilar to previous recessions, students who studied public health, biology, healthcare administration, and other healthcare-related majors received unique luck in finding jobs. Many students opted to work as contact tracers to break into their field until they could find something more fitting once the pandemic settled and the economy stabilized.

How Do Students Move Forward?

While we may want to blame our universities and colleges for not telling us about the best majors for secure employment, or when an economic crash is on the rise, we can't blame them for either. No one can predict an economic downturn, and institutions certainly don't want backlash for telling students to pursue certain degrees resulting in unforeseen unemployment. While there are many things schools could do to better prepare students for life after college, the true responsibility lies in the hands of us, the students. You never know what type of economy you will graduate into, which is why it is exceedingly important to prepare as much as you can. Strengthening your skills, building your network, gaining experiences, and diversifying your résumé to compete with other graduates in the market are necessary preparatory steps. We'll look at many of these techniques later. Ultimately, the only way forward in addressing this intensifying graduate struggle is for students to take their careers into their own hands and become *career savages.*

CHAPTER 2

Your TikTok-Worthy Vacation Can Wait

"We all have dreams. In order to make dreams come
into reality, it takes an awful lot of determination,
dedication, self-discipline, and effort."

—JESSE OWENS

I hated Connecticut. It was such an odd place to live and go
to school. Coming from sunshine and friendly encounters to
unbearable winters and frowning faces was a culture shock
for me. I never imagined myself sitting in a classroom and
looking out the window only to realize I was living in West
Haven, Connecticut, pursuing my bachelor's degree. I always
felt that Los Angeles was a city that provided me with a lot of
external motivation.

I found Connecticut to be a place of complacency. With the
exception of Yale University affiliates, everyone was pretty much
okay with being *okay*. I wasn't used to that type of mindset.
Nonetheless, once I left Los Angeles, I made an unwritten rule
that I would truly experience what Connecticut had to offer
me during that chapter of my life. Throughout my five years in

Connecticut, I flew back to LA three times. Otherwise, I spent every holiday, spring break, and summer vacation working or volunteering. I missed my family and friends but knew the sacrifices I chose to make would result in greater opportunities. As you read on, you will notice that with each experience, I mention deciding to ensure the success of an overall goal, idea, or vision. I consider this form of thinking *foresight*. Many people talk about the importance of hindsight as it allows you to learn from past mistakes, but actionable steps don't stop there. You should be forward-thinking to increase your chances of receiving your desired outcome. The significance of my distaste for Connecticut is less about making California seem more superior and more about drawing attention to my willingness to be uncomfortable in efforts to achieve my definition of success.

Preparing for the Summer After Junior Year

I would have loved to spend the summer before my senior year in Europe eating croissants or in Bali roaming through rice fields like the many people on my Instagram timeline. Unfortunately for me, that was not my fate, but today, I can say I was better off for it. Junior year is almost scarier than senior year. You begin to realize how near the end is. It's nothing more than constant anxiety from the anticipation. I was a frantic person all throughout my junior year. As a result of being a planner with no set plans, my anxiety often crept in. My year of ultimate career-mapping endeavors began at the start of junior year and my first checkbox was securing an internship for the summer. I spent all fall and winter applying then hoping and praying an acceptance would land in my inbox. Despite applying to over one hundred programs, I had not received a single letter in the mail or in my inbox stating, "Congratulations, you'll be interning with XYZ this summer." I didn't even receive a consolation email explaining how many other amazing applicants applied for the opportunity, which made their decision that much harder.

I have always been under the impression that internships are exceedingly hard to get, and I was right. From Columbia University to the University of Southern California, people apply from all over the country. While the name of your university/ college will not matter much by the time you graduate, it is sometimes relevant during the internship application process, especially if you have no professional work experience relevant to your field of study. Internship programs cannot fully gauge the skill set of students, which is why they rely on your GPA, letters of recommendation, school affiliations, and extracurriculars. Think back to when you applied to college. They asked for everything from your social security number to your zip code. You may not think where you went to high school played a role in your acceptance, but it did. High schools are ranked based on the quality of education provided. The metrics used to measure the quality of a high school are grossly inequitable across the nation. A contributing factor is that more privileged communities can afford a host of advantages that result in greater opportunities for the educational enrichment of their students. For example, some schools have standardized test preparation, while other schools may not have the budget for such a thing. Not to mention, standardized state tests play a role in school rankings. With these privileges, some students are granted admission to some of the most prestigious colleges in the nation and so the cycle of privilege and opportunity continues. While my high school was reputable, I didn't feel my college would open internship opportunity doors like Yale University or any other premier college. In my search for an internship, I applied to big companies like Johnson & Johnson and smaller organizations in California and Connecticut to increase my chances, but as time went by, I continued to have zero leads. The more time that passed, the more creatively I began to think.

How am I going to get an internship?

I sat at my laptop, Googling, "how to get an internship," of course, and "working as a pharmacy technician in different states." I tried to transfer my pharmacy technician job to California, but naturally it's illegal to use a Connecticut pharmacy technician license in any state other than Connecticut. I instantly regretted not taking the national exam when my supervisor had advised me to do so. No matter how badly I wanted to go back home, I told myself I couldn't spend an entire summer in LA without a relevant internship opportunity. Logistically, it didn't make sense. Without a structured summer schedule, I knew I would get distracted and potentially derail myself. Working my high school job as an executive assistant to a real estate CEO and CFO was not enough of a reason to go back. I was either staying in Connecticut to work as a pharmacy technician or I would intern within the clinical/medical field in California. I was desperate to spend time outside of West Haven, so I got crafty with my internship application approach.

"Fight or Flight" Your Way into an Internship

In the days leading up to junior year spring break, I was assessing what plans to make. I had $347.52 sitting in my Wells Fargo college checking account after paying my rent, credit card bill, and other utilities. While everyone prepared to head to Panama City Beach, Cabo San Lucas, Miami, and Nassau, I bought a roundtrip economy class ticket to Los Angeles for $300. I felt lame obsessing over finding an internship. All my friends were preparing to have moviesque spring breaks, and I was going home to attempt to find an internship in what felt like the most unorthodox way. My friends always respected my ambitions. They never ridiculed me or purposely made me feel I was missing out on anything. My internship excursion wasn't the first time I opted for my career over making memories with friends, so they were used to my decision-making at this point. On the day of the campus closure, I hitched a ride with my roommate to the Newark New Jersey Airport, and upon arrival, I promptly headed to my gate to board the plane to LAX. I landed in LA early Thursday evening. The moment I stepped out of the terminal, I felt a sense of comfort I hadn't in a while. My mother sat waiting, happy to see I had returned after being away for so long. I ran up to the car, opened the door, and said, "Hi, Mom!"

"How was your flight?" she asked.

I told her how I curated a makeshift internship application packet on my flight.

"Makeshift what? I don't understand what you're saying," she questioned.

I talked her through how I compiled the best parts of my internship application responses and curated a five-page packet for the medical professionals I planned to ask for an internship opportunity. The packet consisted of my one-page résumé, curriculum vitae, and a personal statement detailing why I wanted an internship within the medical field and how the opportunity would further my career journey.

She laughed and said, "Wow. Do you really think that's going to work?"

"I don't know," I said with a chuckle.

I asked my mom to stop at Kinko's on our way home to print out my packets. Of the $47.52 I had left, I spent $27 on printing my makeshift packets and materials. I had twenty-four 8.5 x 11-inch manila envelopes alongside my twenty-four stapled packets. As soon as we pulled into the driveway, I flew out of the car, dropped my luggage at the door, and levitated to my full-sized bed.

After what felt like a restless and anxious sleep, I woke up Friday morning and got dressed in a pair of black slacks, a white button-down, and my favorite pair of J. Crew flats. If I wanted professionals to take me seriously, I needed to dress like one. I made my way out the front door of my mother's house and into my car, only to realize the gas tank was empty. I had $20.52 left in my account and filled the tank with my last dollars. I drove up and down the Pacific Coast Highway and Hawthorne Boulevard, dropping off my packets in the office of every surgeon, clinician, and researcher. For eight hours, I walked and drove all over the South Bay, hoping someone would give me the chance to prove myself. On my way back home, I decided to stop by an isolated internal medicine clinic associated with a well-known Los Angeles university. The receptionists and nurses were talking among themselves as I approached the counter.

One of the nurses asked, "How can I help you?"

"Hello, I'm a pre-med student at the University of New Haven, and I wanted to see if any of the practicing physicians in this facility would be comfortable with me interning for them this summer? I have my CV, résumé, and personal statement here that I can leave for consideration," I recited.

As the receptionist prepared to decline the receipt of my packet, an orthopedic surgeon walked up behind her and said, "We don't allow interns in this facility, but I know there are a few physicians with practices near the hospital up the road who are always very willing to help students."

I perked up my head and thanked the physician for the lead. I never knew private practices surrounded the hospital. As I entered the parking lot, I noticed so many options. To my left was everything from radiology to dermatology, and to my right, a slew of surgical practices. I parked my car and walked into the office of a renowned plastic surgeon within the South Bay and Beverly Hills community. He specialized in breast reconstruction for oncology patients among other general cosmetic procedures. For this story, his name will be Dr. Snider.

"I'm here to see Dr. Snider," I stated.

"Welcome to our office; are you a patient of his?" the receptionist asked.

"No, I'm a pre-med student, and I wanted to know if Dr. Snider had any internship opportunities available?"

The receptionist was taken aback by my directness, not understanding why I needed to speak with the lead surgeon about a nonmedical emergency without an appointment.

"Oh, okay. Let me get the office manager for you," she responded.

The office manager introduced herself and asked me to explain in greater detail what I was looking for. I spoke to her about my interest in plastic surgery and my desire to explore multiple areas within medicine before applying to medical school. While I knew little about Dr. Snider, I expressed how great of an experience it would be to see how a private practice functions in addition to the life of a plastic surgeon. I could tell she was intrigued by my interests and my assertion.

"What's in the packet you provided the receptionist?" she asked.

"Oh! It's a packet detailing my current experience to date and some of the reasons I shared with you about wanting to be a medical intern," I replied.

She skimmed through the packet and said, "Great! I'll take this and provide it to Dr. Snider. Email me on Monday to follow up."

She handed me her business card, and I walked out of the office, feeling exhausted and relieved all at the same time. I was one step closer to securing an internship.

The weekend rolled by, and before I knew it, it was Monday morning. I quickly opened my laptop and began writing into Dr. Snider's office to follow up on my request. I submitted my email at 8:00 a.m. and received a response from the office manager at 8:45 a.m. My one-on-one with Dr. Snider was scheduled for Tuesday. She mentioned in her email that Dr. Snider would like to meet with me before deciding. I spent the rest of Monday thinking of responses to questions he may ask me. If he asked me why plastic surgery, I planned to detail the importance of self-image and confidence and its direct relationship with mental health. If he asked me what I enjoy most about being a pre-med student, I planned to discuss the excitement of studying an ever-evolving field.

On Tuesday morning, I drove back down to the private practice reflecting on how one crazy idea was going to become a reality. I was escorted to Dr. Snider's office within two minutes of checking in with the receptionist. After fifteen minutes, Dr. Snider walked in and introduced himself.

"Hi Ruqayyah, I'm Dr. Snider. I've heard a lot about you."

I got up and said, "Thank you for taking the time to meet with me."

His office manager joined the conversation as we discussed my pharmacy technician experience and my desire to explore multiple areas of medicine before locking in on my career plans. I discussed my difficulty in finding an internship which led me to his office. The conversation ebbed and flowed for twenty minutes before he stopped me mid-sentence and expressed his great desire to help students decide what they want to do with their lives.

"I became a doctor to help patients, but I am also in this profession to help students. That's why I am going to let you intern with me for the summer. You may leave this internship and realize surgery isn't for you, or maybe just plastic surgery isn't for you, and that's okay. What I do want is for you to have an opportunity to experience what you don't know before committing to a life of medicine."

I was elated. We shook hands, and the office manager said she would provide the next steps via email. I went from struggling to find a summer internship to being offered a surgical intern position with a plastic surgeon. While I was jealous of all the fun I saw my friends having on social media, missing spring break was worth the sacrifice.

As I mentioned earlier, while you navigate your career, you should remember to always be forward-thinking. The phenomenon of graduating with no experience starts with this scenario. My extreme desire to get an internship resulted from thinking I wouldn't be a competitive applicant when I applied to medical school. You get to junior year and think an internship won't make or break future opportunities, but it will. Building upon my scientific/clinical experience began with this internship. As you go through college, no matter what stage you are in, make it a priority to gain career experiences, paid or not. The exposure will allow employers to feel more comfortable offering you a paid position and you to gauge your career interests.

If no one has ever told you this, let me be the first to say, "You miss all the shots you don't take in life." A large percentage of people fear putting themselves in uncomfortable and unpredictable situations because they fear rejection. The downside to fear of rejection is the reality that it stems from a lack of confidence, but on the upside, you can work toward building that confidence. A higher level of confidence will allow you to take more risks that may result in career advancement, among other things. When you value yourself, your view of rejection is less about the other party not wanting any association with you and more about the mutual relationship not being seen as beneficial for either of you. If a job or internship "rejects" you, all this means is it was not the right position for you. I guarantee you; the right opportunity will always come at the right time. We will touch more on self-value and confidence throughout this guide.

If I didn't put myself out there while looking for an internship, I would have spent the summer of 2015 internship-less! When it comes to looking for a job or an internship, sometimes you have to adopt unorthodox practices to get what you want. I call these practices "Savage Strategies." There will always be people in your field of interest who want to help you, and sometimes, all you have to do is ask. Dr. Snider was not looking for a surgical intern. There were no internship postings for his practice. He cultivated the opportunity for me not only because I asked but also because he has dedicated himself to helping students interested in medicine. The entire summer, I was the only intern working in Dr. Snider's private practice and proudly so. If you are looking for an internship, I want to challenge you to reach out to people in your field as I did. I strongly suggest walking into the offices of the professionals you are interested in interning for. While you can send an email, entering the office of your potential mentor can initiate an immediate connection.

Finding an Internship, the "Savage" Way:

1. Reach out to at least twenty different professionals in your field. (e.g., If you are interested in law, reach out to twenty lawyers or private practices and ask if they are interested in having a summer intern. Similarly, if you are interested in digital marketing, you would be surprised how an Instagram, Tik Tok or Twitter direct message can turn into a summer social media internship for your favorite local brand/business.)

2. Reach out to ten people on LinkedIn. Whether it be with an elder peer or an established professional, chances are, you can gain an internship opportunity from someone in your LinkedIn network. If one of the connections you reach out to cannot help you, they might be able to connect you with someone who can.

3. Upload your résumé to job platforms. Indeed, CareerBuilder, Glassdoor, Zip Recruiter, and Monster aren't just for applying to jobs. Upload your résumé on these platforms and tag it with "intern," "internship," "summer internship," "summer intern," and any other tags you think apply. Additionally, turn on the "Open to Opportunities" feature on your LinkedIn profile!

4. Apply for internships the normal way. You want to make sure all your bases are covered. Give yourself a weekly goal on how many internships you want to apply to and reward yourself when the goal is met.

5. Follow up. Until you get a "no," follow up with all the professionals you reach out to. Don't feel like you are bothering them. A good rule of thumb is after three attempts you can assume they don't have the bandwidth to take on an intern.

Here is a sample email you should send when reaching out to people in your field:

SUBJECT LINE: [Insert University/College Name Here] Student Seeking Summer Internship

Dear [Insert Name and Title] or To Whom It May Concern:

I hope this email finds you well. My name is [Insert Your First and Last Name Here] and I am an upcoming senior at [Insert University/College Name Here] majoring in [Insert Major Here]. I have taken great interest in [Insert Subject Matter Here] and believe I can learn a great deal from you as I plan for the next steps in my career. I am expected to graduate [Expected Graduation Date] and want to expose myself to all aspects of this profession before doing so. I have read up on your background and would like to ask if you are open to having a summer intern. I can execute all duties thrown my way as I am a fast learner and believe the best way to learn is through robust experience. Lastly, I believe being in this environment would enrich the education I have received thus far. For reference, I have attached my résumé/CV and hope to hear from you soon.

Sincerely,

[Insert Your First and Last Name Here]

[Insert Your Major and Minor Here]

[Insert Your Email Here]

[Insert Your Number Here]

The Beauty of Thinking Outside the Box

My internship began immediately after my junior year concluded. Before doing anything, Dr. Snider requested that I fill out observer paperwork with the local memorial hospital. I originally avoided asking the hospital for an internship because I assumed they would have an abundance of interns already. To my surprise, he was an affiliate of the hospital. He and his colleagues of different specialties all performed various surgeries within the facility. I was thrilled to know I would be seeing patients in his private practice and observing surgeries at one of the larger hospitals in the South Bay region of Los Angeles.

This internship was an excellent medical opportunity for me. I spent the first month with a general surgeon who specialized in bariatric surgery, incorporating laparoscopic and robotic techniques in gastrointestinal surgeries. The next month, my observations consisted of rhinoplasties, breast reconstructions/augmentations, and various other plastic surgeries performed by Dr. Snider. Additionally, I saw patients who authorized my presence during initial and follow-up examinations. The more I interacted with surgeons, primary care physicians, patients, and medical staff, the more my perception of pursuing medicine changed.

Midway through my internship, I attended a lap band removal and gastric bypass surgery. It was a notable experience. This was my sixth gastric bypass observation, and after leaving the operating room, I knew general surgery could never be something I pursued. I stepped out of the room after two and a half hours, removed my mask, and washed my hands and arms for two minutes. There was a thirty-minute break before my next observation. I followed all the surgeons into the break room for some food, coffee, and conversation. I sat in a corner sipping my cappuccino, watching the surgeons interact with each other, discussing each of their caseloads. A five-foot-tall African American woman walked into the room and commanded the attention of all her colleagues. She greeted each of them with a subtle wave and sat next to me.

"Are you a medical student?" she asked.

"No, I'm just shadowing a few surgeons before I go back to college. I'll be a senior this year."

She grabbed my hand and asked, "Do you really want to become a surgeon?"

"I think so," I said reluctantly.

Before standing up and quietly exiting the room, she paused, looked me in my eyes, and said, "Don't do it for the money. You'll never be happy, and honestly, most of us miss out on the greatest moments in life because we decided to devote our lives to surgery. I enjoy my job. I don't do it for the money, and you shouldn't either."

Her colleagues chimed in and joined the conversation agreeing with her stance. The twenty minutes they spent trying to deter me from pursuing surgery felt like hours.

One surgeon said, "Take it from me, having a family while pursuing surgery is difficult," while looking out the window watching the Los Angeles rain hit the asphalt. The moment felt dramatic, but I could sense the message the surgeon was trying to portray.

"And the student loans for medical school are unbelievable," another surgeon proclaimed.

At the end of the conversation, everyone dispersed, and I was left sitting in the corner, coffee still in hand. I got up, walked out the door, and went to my next observation. Everything they had to say played in my mind throughout the entire double mastectomy procedure. I asked myself if the truth of their words meant medicine wasn't for me. When you become an intern in the field you believe you want to pursue, you will have conversations like the ones I had with professionals in the field. The talks did not deter me wholeheartedly but rather provided me with insight.

I have been around many clinicians, and I always know there is a fifty-fifty chance someone will tell me not to pursue medicine. The thing is, when you have a vision you are passionate about, the advice of others (alongside their shared experiences) can influence you, but that does not mean your desire to pursue aspects of your professional vision will go away. During your internship, be open to hearing what people have to say. You may realize that the career you thought you wanted is not exactly how you pictured it. You may realize the specialty you wanted to pursue is no longer of interest. Learn to accept that changes to your ultimate plan are okay. An internship is invaluable. Some people graduate college and experience their field of study for the first time. They end up bouncing around in different areas of their industry, trying to figure out what they enjoy. With an internship, you place yourself in a great position to decide sooner than later. Even if you are simply narrowing down your options by interning, you are setting yourself up for greater success.

I spent a few days thinking about what the surgeons had to say. I recall driving to my internship one morning with my mom while my car was in the shop. "All of the surgeons basically told me not to become a doctor," I told her.

"Why would they say that?" my mother shouted in frustration. I could tell the guidance of these surgeons was interfering with her vision for me.

"Well, they talked about the sacrifices they all had to make and that I shouldn't do it just for the money," I softly blurted. I was irritated by my mother's outrage. It was as if she couldn't tell I was trying to understand the advice and figure out how to best apply it to better my career and life.

She abruptly stopped at a red light and said, "I don't think these people should be discouraging students like this."

"Mom, I don't think they are saying I can't do. I think they were trying to get me to understand the risks. I *did* want to pursue plastic surgery because they make the most money, but I have to want to pursue that path for more than just money."

For the remainder of the car ride, she lectured me about becoming a doctor, taking the MCAT on time, and applying before senior year was over. She asked about letters of recommendation and if Dr. Snider would write one for me. My mother was in complete denial that it was possible I wouldn't go down the surgical route or the medical school route, for that matter. With most things, if I doubt myself, my mom will reinforce how capable I am, but this was different. It wasn't self-doubt. It was me taking in my internship experience and realizing I may have been interested in my preferred profession in medicine for the wrong reasons. The entire conversation was added pressure I didn't need. Outside of my internship, I was stressed from my summer schedule alone. Every day for three months, I would wake up at 5:30 a.m. and prepare for the day ahead of me.

6:00–6:30 a.m.: arrive at the hospital to prepare for surgical observation

7:00–12:00 p.m.: see patients or continue to observe surgical procedures

12:30–5:30 p.m.: work at Keller Williams Realty as the executive assistant to the CEO/CFO

6:00 p.m.–12:00 a.m.: network and research potential jobs to apply for before graduation

12:00–5:30 a.m.: sleep

To a certain degree, I mentally muted my mom's voice. Her stance only made me feel more conflicted. We pulled into the parking lot of Dr. Snider's office. I got out and mumbled my goodbye. Before I could sit down, I was called into an exam room to watch the doctor redress a patient's wounds post-procedure. I stood in the corner, and I could feel the twelve-by-twelve-foot room spinning. A bullet of sweat raced down my face and into my eye. I was hot and suddenly nauseous. I quietly excused myself and rushed through the lobby and out into the parking lot. I paced up and down the lot, hyperventilating and using my hands as fans for my face.

I questioned, "What the hell is happening to me?"

It felt as if I had an out-of-body experience. I immediately called a friend and she asked what happened leading up to this feeling. We discussed the conversation with my mom, and she immediately knew I had my first panic attack. Senior year and the stress of what's to come for your future can do this to you. I mention this experience to assure you that you are not alone. The conversation with my mother was layered with so many decisions I wasn't ready to make, especially in light of accepting my internship experience for what it was. If you feel panicky about the future, take a moment to breathe and understand that stressing does nothing. If you have trouble regulating your stress on your own, talk to a friend. I guarantee your friends have felt the same way too.

The Importance of Internships

We have come a long way from students not caring about internship opportunities to applying for as many as possible. The National Association of Colleges and Employers found that 50 percent of the 2008 graduating class had internship opportunities compared to the 17 percent of graduates from 1992. Despite the number of graduates increasing, the number of graduates with internship experience is not increasing at the same rate. From 2008 to now, only 57.5 percent of students who receive job offers completed an internship before graduating. The slow growth in students gaining internship opportunities before entering the workforce could be a key factor in why many graduates struggle to gain post-graduation employment in their field of study. Internships are often a deciding factor between two candidates. It's the exact amount of experience employers desire to see before making an offer. More importantly, interns create opportunities for themselves during their internships. The majority of interns receive full-time offers from the organizations they interned for. Internships also allow students to decipher between certain roles within their field. If you work as an accounting intern learning daily accounting tasks and activities, you can later decide you don't desire a career in the world of accounting. From there, you can make an informed decision and pursue other job opportunities within your field. You can do a million other things with an accounting degree. Overall, an internship broadens your knowledge, allows you to make more informed career choices, and makes you more of a competitive applicant.

What Do Internships Teach You?

At the end of my internship, I decided I no longer wanted to pursue surgery, but I knew that didn't mean I would forgo clinical work altogether. I personally thanked each person I interacted with, from the receptionist to the surgeons, with a card or a personalized email. My summer interning for Dr. Snider truly altered my perception and I was greatly appreciative of each person I worked with. When I first walked into his office at the start of summer, he said, "You may like plastic surgery now, but slow down and see what else the medical field has to offer you. I never want students prematurely making career choices." He ended up being right.

Outside gaining experience, your internship has a lot to offer. This will not be the first time you see me highlight the importance of networking. I connected with many healthcare professionals during my internship who educated me on ways a biology major can excel in the medical setting without having a doctorate. Had it not been for these additional connections, I would have continued to navigate my career lacking important information. Holding onto my belief in maintaining my network for future benefits, I made sure to keep in touch with Dr. Snider in the coming months and years, updating him on where I was in my career and where I saw myself going. As a result of my maintaining the relationship, he was honored to write me a letter of recommendation. Additionally, when a friend of mine was looking for medical exposure, I connected her with Dr. Snider, and he took her on as an intern too! If I had gone to medical school, graduated, and completed my residency, I truly believe Dr. Snider would have guided me through finding employment. There are many ways an internship connection can manifest into other opportunities. When you conclude your internship, be sure to send a thank-you letter or email to your mentor/supervisor and any other pertinent staff who may have offered you additional learning experiences during your program. After sending thank-you letters, connect with each person on LinkedIn to ensure you don't forget you once interacted with that person.

I learned a lot during my internship. Not only did I learn what a rhinoplasty was, but I also learned a lot about myself. I spent my entire summer working and interning and realized I needed to let some opportunities go to focus on others. That summer was the last time I worked my high school job. Many people like to leave that option open should they want to return post-graduation. I was never going to see real estate through and felt it was a comfortable distraction. At the start of summer, I set one goal for myself: to quit my CVS job upon arrival in Connecticut. Of course, I wasn't going to quit without having another employment opportunity lined up. I managed to apply, interview, and accept a job offer from a local hospital two towns over from my university all while working and interning (more on this in Chapter 3). My first week on the job synced with the first week of campus opening for senior year.

Summer of Goals

Setting goals during each stage of your life gives you a better aim. You need to know what you are shooting for so you can properly work toward achieving your goals. I want you to take a moment to think of some goals for the summer. What do you want to accomplish before matriculating into your final year of college? What goals are going to better prepare you for graduation day?

Here is a list of suggestions as you create your savage summer goals:

Kyyah's Savage Summer Goals:

1. Intern for a medical professional
2. Work to maintain financial freedom
3. Research potential roles in medical industry
4. Complete/update LinkedIn profile and connect with biotech,science, and pharma recruiters weekly
5. Update résumé and upload onto job search platforms

Other goals to consider:

- Beginning graduate school applications
- Study for the GMAT
- Compile letters of recommendation
- Volunteer
- Map out business objectives
- Finding a new part-time job in Connecticut

My Savage Summer Goals:

1)

2)

3)

4)

5)

The Prepared Graduate

PART II

SENIOR YEAR

CHAPTER 3

The Year of Lasts

"It's hard work that makes things happen."
—SHONDA RHIMES

When I was preparing to go away to college, I dragged my mother to Target to buy me XL-twin-size bedding and a whole bunch of other nonsense I didn't need. I mean, who needs a pizza cutter in their dorm room? Senior year was a completely different shopping experience. My roommates and I opted to purchase our beds off Craigslist, our couch from Goodwill, and we made a coffee table out of wooden crates we found on the side of the road. I lived approximately five hundred feet away from campus, which made coming up with commute excuses to skip class during the winter season nearly impossible. I was excited for senior year. It was going to be the year of lasts: my last homecoming, last spring weekend, and the last time I would get to live under the same roof with all my friends from college. I was ready to attend every football game and every fraternity party within the tri-state area—that is, until I got home from my first week of classes.

I lived with three of my closest friends in a three-bedroom duplex. Our living room was massive, so we converted it into a fourth bedroom to cut down on the cost of rent per person. For this story, I am going to call my roommates Noelle, Liana, and Kasey. Noelle and I each worked two jobs senior year—one related to our majors and another to supplement our income. We were both professionally aligned and would end our long weeks together, sitting on the couch with a glass of red wine and conversation.

"Girl, I need to find a job," Noelle said one day. I was puzzled by her statement and told her she didn't need a third job when she already had two. "I'm talking about one for after graduation," she replied.

As I took a sip of my wine, I looked at her and said, "First semester just started; you'll find a job."

"Yeah, I hope so, but until then, I'm not going out like that. I spent the last three years partying like college is free."

"What do you mean?"

"We raged as freshmen, were reckless as sophomores, and we turned up Wednesday through Sunday all junior year. We don't need to do that anymore. I don't feel the need to go out every single night," she said. She went on to say, "I never had to worry about entering the real world as a freshman, sophomore, or junior. Senior year isn't a game. Sure, there's all this fun stuff happening on campus but, girl, you know what isn't fun?"

"What?" I asked.

"Not having a job after spending four years in West Haven and moving back into my mom's house after having all the freedom in the world," she explained. I nodded my head in complete agreement and realization.

Noelle was right. The excitement of activities on campus isn't directed toward seniors. It is at each student's discretion to decide what to go to and what to pass up on. Sure, I would miss everything about college, from the sports to my friends, but my last year wasn't the time for me to get caught up in the sea of campus activities. I needed to pick my focus and stay the course.

Pick Your Focus

Don't become distracted by the number of things taking place on campus. Attend events and enjoy your senior year but remember to focus on the bigger picture. Freshman, sophomores, and juniors can run the risk of being reckless. They enroll in another year of classes, whereas you will matriculate into either the realm of corporate America, a graduate program (which is unlike undergrad), or the complexity of entrepreneurship. Senior year will fly by quicker than any other year, and you will need to spend your "last" first and second semesters preparing for what's to come, especially if you failed to complete an internship or make the time to network within your field during the summer. Starting senior year jobless or internship-less means you need to make tremendous progress in completing your savage summer goals (see Chapter 2) in addition to the steps outlined in this chapter. At this current moment, you decide what your primary focus will be senior year: approaching the "lasts" of your college experience with the similar mindset of a freshman or focusing on setting yourself up for a successful entrance into the next stage of your life.

Phase 1: Operation Relevant Experience

It may have appeared that my summer solely consisted of interning and working, but I was crafting my master plan as well. I needed to reevaluate my employment to avoid eating different renditions of Top Ramen upon my return to school. I was making $11 an hour and knew with a rent increase I'd have to make more money or go back to three-for-one-dollar dinners. With that in mind, all summer, I went back and forth attempting to renegotiate my hourly rate. I was unsuccessful in winning that battle. Beyond the money, I strongly disliked working for CVS. Working within a retail pharmacy is an extremely stressful job. You must meet dozens of patients' demands at once while manning three stations singlehandedly. I had to ask myself five important questions before running the risk of quitting and entertaining another job offer. During college and thereafter, you will run into similar dilemmas: a job you hate or pay you can no longer accept. Just as I did, these are the questions you should ask yourself when debating if leaving a job you currently have is the right decision:

1. Am I still learning at this job?
2. Am I happy at this job?
3. Do I feel I can grow at this job?
4. Am I making enough to support myself?
5. Will working here continue to help me reach my overall career goal?

If you answered "no" to any or all of these questions, it might be time to forge forward. At the start of summer, I applied to a local hospital to work as a pharmacy technician. They were slow in responding to my emails, which led to me calling once or twice a week to check on the status of my application. Three weeks before senior year, I decided to inform my superiors at CVS that I would no longer be working there. I was confident I would receive an offer from the local hospital after my initial phone interview, and I was right. They asked me to come in for an in-person interview forcing me to leave my internship and part-time job two weeks early. Keep in mind, my summer earnings were not spent on frivolous things. I saved nearly 80 percent of my earnings in case I ended up jobless. Take risks but be smart about it. Obviously, having no job means no income, and a lack of income equals a decrease in overall quality of life. Some of you may have parents who will financially support you in times of distress, but if not, you need to think strategically about how you spend your money. The hospital offered me the job two days after my interview. I went from $11 to $15 per hour. Leaving CVS was the right call.

This is why I tell all Career Savage clients: high risk equals high reward. When you take risks and believe in yourself, you are more likely to reach your maximum potential. Stop wasting your time working in places you hate. Many people do this after graduating, and you should get into the habit of *not* doing that now. If you work at a pizza place and you are a microbiology major, I have a question for you. Why are you working there? Don't say, "I need the money." This kind of mindset is dangerous. Even if you do need the money, try to find jobs that allow you to do both, make money and advance in your career. You are either passionate about pizza or you are passionate about microbiology. Why work in an establishment that contributes absolutely nothing to your career? If pizza is your passion, change your major to culinary arts and stay where you are because you're doing great (said in Kris Jenner's voice). If you would prefer to work in a lab preparing smears, you can make that happen for yourself. Don't sell yourself short by believing you aren't qualified to apply. The first semester has started and it's not too late to contact labs and local hospitals for an opportunity. You would be surprised how basic the requirements are for certain laboratory technician positions. No offense to laboratory technicians. I know some of you reading this won't believe this is possible, so here are the general position qualifications for a hospital laboratory technician (requirements will vary per medical facility):

- Candidates are required to have a high school diploma or GED.
  - ✓ Look at that! You have one of those. Can't start college without it.
- Must have some background knowledge of laboratory practices and/or experience.
  - ✓ Look at that! You have that too. Your science lectures are paired with labs.
- Must have good communication skills and be able to work in a group setting.
  - ✓ If you have ever worked on a group project and did moderately well, you have good communication skills. There's no greater challenge than a group project.
- Must have extensive computer skills.
  - ✓ If you have a smartphone and know how to use it, you have computer skills. They are basically minicomputers.
- Candidate must be self-driven and assertive to successfully perform the duties defined above.
  - ✓ If you feel comfortable calling hospitals and labs as instructed here, you *are* more self-driven and assertive than you may think.

I know some people truly have no choice and need to work odd jobs to pay their bills. The tips I am providing here are simply a guideline you should try to follow. Remember, no advice is mandatory. I would like to draw your attention to one major that can get away with working anywhere, and that's a business major. No matter where they work, business majors can spin their experience to their benefit. Every establishment is a business; therefore, every experience is relevant. Let's say Sally Savage is a senior majoring in business administration, working at a local arts and crafts store as a sales associate. While Sally can simply list her cashier duties, this is what Sally should have on her résumé under that experience to highlight her business experience:

Sales Associate
Hidden Valley Arts & Crafts

- Assess customers' needs, provide assistance, and information on product features
- Strategize ways to improve sales (e.g., planning marketing activities, changing the store's design)
- Exceed department's sales goals monthly and quarterly
- Cross-sell products
- Maintain quality customer service
- Process POs

Sally worked at this craft store all senior year, and because of that, she easily received employment upon graduating. Sally landed her a job at an interior design firm as a business development associate. The essential responsibilities of a business development associate are:

- Drive sales to meet and exceed set goals
- Develop repeat business and maintain client relationships
- Maintain the showroom's organization and aesthetics

So how did Sally land this job opportunity? First, while working at Hidden Valley, she was required to meet sales goals each month and each quarter. When applying for this job, she informed the employer of her track record when ensuring sales goals were met. Second, developing repeat business and maintaining client relationships was another important role Sally played while working at Hidden Valley. She told the employer she knows the importance of client relationships and how frequently artists came into her store simply to engage and seek her advisement before a purchase. She mentioned that her customers trusted her. Third, at Hidden Valley, she was responsible for changing the store's design to improve the sale of certain products. Sally ensured the employer she understood aesthetics were pertinent in making sales. The one road bump Sally thought she would run into was the minimum requirement of two-year sales experience. She thought she only had one, forgetting she served as a sales associate at Forever 21 and the UPS store during her earlier college years. This hypothetical scenario is an example showing why business majors can work anywhere.

The main takeaway is you should stop working jobs that don't contribute to your career advancement. Be the microbiology major who works in a microbiology lab. Be the culinary major who works in a pizza shop. Be just like Sally Savage. With graduation around the corner, a lack of experience is exactly why employers will not hire you. Most students in your graduating class will receive a degree come May. What sets you apart from anyone else with a college degree? Nothing, except real-life professional experience. You probably aren't thinking of having kids anytime soon, but think about this for a second: would you entrust the life of your newborn child with someone who has raised healthy and happy children of their own, or would you entrust your newborn with someone who went to school for nannying? I mean, someone who has never actually watched a child but has read *How to Nanny 101*. I don't know about you, but I am entrusting my child to a person with real-life experience.

People who intern and work in fields related to their major are the ones who land the relevant jobs come graduation day, and not because they had a 4.0. Understand that any job you get after graduation will have on-the-job training. This is why GPAs are no more than a number. Employers want to know you can hit the ground running in a professional setting. They want to know you are capable of learning quickly and bringing innovative thought processes to the table. They couldn't care less that you paid someone to write your English papers, among other things, to maintain that high GPA.

When I got my first big pharma job, I was not exactly clear about regulatory affairs. My recruiter told me point-blank they were offering me the job because of my experience as a pharmacy technician. Though a degree in science was required for the position, no one looked at my GPA or even cared that I had a bachelor's in science. All that mattered was that I had a degree and the experience. When I got to the job, everything (and I mean everything) was on-the-job training. My degree gave me fundamental knowledge in understanding human biology and its relation to the pharmacokinetics and pharmacodynamics of pharmaceutical products, but my work experience allowed me to better comprehend my training. Some of you may think it is crazy to think GPAs do not matter, especially because we are taught to believe this number determines our probability of success. Let me clarify for those interested in pursuing medical school, law school, or graduate school. For those applications, your grade point average matters. For those of you interested in entering the workforce after graduation, it does not matter as much. Of all the phases we will discuss in this chapter, gaining relevant work experience is the most important thing. Make sure you make this a priority senior year.

Phase 2: Operation Social Media

Social media is a blessing and a curse. On one end, you can connect with people and build your network. It grants you the potential to advance in your career and/or further your entrepreneurial efforts. At the other end, you may find yourself riddled with anxiety and slight depression watching your peers appear to be living luxurious and interesting lives. Even though at this point we all know social media is *not* a true depiction of real life, our minds still allow us to believe otherwise. Attempting to not compare yourself to others can be challenging. You ask yourself, "How is [*insert applicable name here*] able to do this during senior year? Is their major less rigorous?" Regardless of the questions you are asking yourself, never forget social media is not a true reflection of people's lives. For *years* people assumed I did nothing but travel, and I can't blame them, as I portrayed my life to be that way. Some people would even question if I was a student because I never posted anything related to my studies. Well, public service announcement: I have student loans to prove I was in school. My life, your life, and everyone else's are never as it appears to be online because we all choose to showcase the highlights of our life experiences.

During this semester, you need to work on developing a healthy relationship with social media. Refrain from falling victim to the comparison game and direct your energies toward using social media to benefit your professional growth. Take a moment to think about how social media benefits your life and the pros and cons of consistently engaging.

Social Media Use	
Pros	Cons

As you reflect on why you utilize these social platforms, think of other applications you feel may do your career more justice. Millennials and Generation Z are fluent in Tik Tok, YouTube, Snapchat, Instagram, and Facebook. It's almost as if engaging on such platforms is second nature. While these programs serve a great recreational (and sometimes professional) purpose, LinkedIn is the number one platform you should be well-versed in senior year and thereafter. I promise you: LinkedIn is far more beneficial for your professional development and mental health. My first semester of senior year, I spent a great deal of my time networking on LinkedIn. As a result, I could leverage my network later in my career. The saying, "It's not what you know but who you know," is the only superannuated piece of advice I still follow.

After learning the benefits of LinkedIn, I chose to update my profile even when I had only achieved the smallest goals. It didn't matter if I attended a conference or completed an additional hour of volunteer work; my connections would see the progress I was making as a working professional. In addition to frequently updating my LinkedIn profile, I spent a great deal of time messaging random people within the medical industry, asking for advice on how they got to where they were at the time. I set up coffee meetings with hospital residents and phone calls with various clinical professionals, simply to learn more than I already knew. LinkedIn was, and still is, the best place to advance your network. LinkedIn is still a social media platform, but you often see more authenticity.

Amid executing my idea of social networking strategies, I occasionally scrolled on Instagram only to find my peers dressed in costumes attending the latest themed parties or traveling the world. One of my classmates was infamous for traveling to a new country every other week. For this example, I will refer to her as

Carrie. I was perplexed at how *great* Carrie's life appeared to be. I imagined she was passing her classes, locked down a job offer, and was enjoying all that senior year had to offer. How else was she so lax with gradation around the corner? I was stressed, and she was sipping mai-tais on the beach of Cocotal, Dominican Republic. Here is the kicker: at the end of our first semester, rumors circulated that Carrie would not be returning to campus in the spring. To my surprise, she was funding her extravagant celebrity-like vacations with her financial aid funds. Before I continue, I must advise you don't become a victim to luxury by purchasing experiences and items you cannot afford in the presence of an educational loan. Additionally, using student loans for anything other than academia only leaves you on the opposite side of a rude awakening. Carrie missed so many classes she was unable to keep up with assignments and pass exams. She did not graduate with my class and left to collect her diploma at a much later date.

It's important to enjoy your senior year, but do not get caught up the same way Carrie did. Do not be distracted from focusing on the big picture because your Instagram timeline and TikTok feed are pressuring you. More importantly, refrain from comparing yourself to your peers on social platforms. That advice is for senior year *and* for the rest of your life. The outcome of Carrie's escapades should be enough proof to know that *not all that glitters is gold*. I want you to spend the rest of senior year asking yourself, how will [insert action] benefit me in the future? How will this [insert action] contribute to my life, for the better, after college? You won't be a senior forever, so it's time to broaden your way of thinking and do better than Carrie.

Let's face it: Instagram and TikTok are the most popular and most used social media platforms among Millennials and Generation Z. As Instagram and TikTok continue to evolve, you will begin to see how they can benefit your future. However, you must alter your perception of *what* social media means to you. As I previously stated, it should not be used to compare yourself and your career status to others but rather to acquire information that feeds your professional and personal development. Millennials and Generation Z have a high probability of suffering from mental illness due to extended social media use. It's hard to cultivate a healthy relationship with platforms so easily accessible by the press of a button. When you form a healthy relationship with social media, you will begin to realize how it can be used to grow your business and personal brand instead of your ego.

For example, while sending people DMs on social media has become somewhat overrated, for many reasons, this small feature holds a world of possibilities. If people used social media for networking and acquiring information rather than "stunting" and "flexing" for external validation, I guarantee you there would be a larger number of people who are ahead in their careers. And there would also be far fewer people left to suffer from anxiety and/or depression. Even though the idea may sound uncomfortable, sending a DM to someone in your professional field will likely generate a lead or an opportunity. Hundreds of doctors, lawyers, sound engineers, singers, rappers, pharmacists, models, entrepreneurs, graduate students, actresses, actors, bloggers, scientists, writers, photographers, nurses, police officers, and so many other professionals would be thrilled to answer any career questions you have. They would delineate why they chose their career path and what you should do to get to where they are. Some may even offer an internship or job opportunity should you continue to engage with them regularly. You may think there is no use in sending a message to a stranger because the likelihood of someone answering a DM on social media is slim, but you'd be surprised. It only takes one person to open the door to opportunity.

If the person you are reaching out to has all three social media accounts, this means you have three ways of getting in contact with them and getting the information you need. You can also use this same strategy to look for a job. It is as easy as opening a social media app, searching for what you are looking for, and sending one person or a few people a message. When you send people messages on social media, the first thing they will do after reading the message is check your social media profile. This is why you must clean your profiles before reaching out to people you wish to build professional relationships with.

Every social media platform you use needs to undergo what I call *social media spring cleaning*. If you think employers and graduate institutions don't Google you before an interview or review of your application, you're wrong. Almost every employer of mine has Googled or done a LinkedIn search prior to speaking with me in greater detail, and I don't doubt they will do the same to you. I have learned early on that everything on the internet is connected. For this reason, I use different names for different things. For example, family, close friends, and professionals in my career field call me Ruqayyah, while acquaintances and Career Savage clients call me Kyyah. None of my social media platforms are linked to my real name apart from my LinkedIn profile. When employers search "Ruqayyah Abdulrahoof," the first thing that pops up is my LinkedIn profile. Next are all articles and pages related to my profession. I search my name once a year to ensure no information I disapprove of appears and occasionally I stumble upon dubious background check websites that provide personal details.

Some may believe reviewing the background check websites that come up when you search your name is excessive. Especially when employers run their own checks after making candidates job offers. Nonetheless, some of the information on these sites are extremely personal and should not be so easily accessible by anyone with a computer or smartphone. One website listed all my previous addresses and my siblings' names, ages, and where they presently resided. To combat the circulation of my information, I periodically contact background check websites and request the removal of personal details. It's as simple as calling or emailing with the request to remove your data. I never know what they will post and how it may jeopardize my career. If you search your name and face the same issues, use the guide below when contacting the site.

How to Get a Background Check Website to Remove Your Information

The conversation should go something like this:

Dial the 1-800 number or customer service number published on their website

Customer Service Rep: Thank you for calling [insert company name], a website that posts and sells personal profiles of people without their knowledge or permission. How may I help you?

You: Hello, I am calling to have my personal information removed from your website.

Customer Service Rep: Do you have an account with us?

You: No, I do not have an account, but my personal information is publicly posted, and I have not authorized your website to display my information. I am requesting my profile be removed.

Customer Service Rep: I am so sorry about that, blah blah blah. All I need is your name and age, and I can proceed with the removal.

You: My first name is [blank], and I am [blank] years old.

Customer Service Rep: Thank you for that; I have submitted your request. It will take twenty-four to forty-eight hours to be removed from our site and five to seven business days to be removed from Google and other search engines. May I help you with anything else?

You: No, thank you. I will follow up in seven days should my profile still be public. Have a great day.

Customer Service Rep: Thank you for calling [insert company name]. Have a great day.

My YouTube channels, Twitter, Pinterest, Instagram, TikToks, Facebook, and Snapchat are all separate from my professional life. During year two of Career Savage, I went to many networking events in Los Angeles to get the brand's name out there. During one of the events, I met a male high school teacher who started a motivational firm to inspire youth with troubled backgrounds. Let's call him Tom. Tom and I had a great conversation on motivating youth and equipping them with confidence to achieve their dreams. As is usual in Los Angeles culture, we exchanged Instagram handles. Of course, I was present as Kyyah Abdul, Career Savage strategist, so I gave him the Career Savage Instagram rather than my personal one. A few days later, I received a direct message from Tom asking to reconnect and have a follow-up discussion regarding our two businesses. We spoke over Instagram video and before the conversation concluded, Tom stated he found my personal Instagram and thought it was a completely different person. That is how separate I keep my personal life, Career Savage, and professional life. Call me paranoid, but I don't want employers seeing all the workout infographics and cocktail mixing guides I have pinned to my Pinterest page. To give you more perspective, here is what my social media realm looks like:

	Personal	Career Savage	Professional (Medical/Public Health Career & Academia)
Alias	Kyyah, Kyyah Abdul	Kyyah Abdul	Ruqayyah Abdulrahoof
Accounts	@kyyahabdul on Instagram, Tiktok, YouTube, Twitter, and Pinterest Facebook Snapchat ThoughtCatalog.com	CareerSavage.com @careersavage on Instagram, TikTok, YouTube, and Twitter	LinkedIn
What gets posted?	Personal photos Travel photos Workout inspiration Rants Fashion Skincare routines Blog-esque content Healthy food ideas VLOGs Relationships	Career advice Career inspiration Career motivation Career fashion	Public health topics Medical topics Health topics Academia Professional updates

If you want to get crazy with cleaning up your digital trace, clean up your Venmo, or at the least, make your transactions private. Putting the smoke emoji and a tree emoji to pay the same person every other week certainly points to patterns you don't want people in the professional world to know. You may be thinking, "But, you can't Google a person's Venmo transaction history—it is only accessible to mutual friends who use the app."

Yes, you are indeed correct, but let me tell you, the world is smaller than you may like to believe. You never know who knows whom and how your information could fall into the hands of your future employer or their current employees. For those of you who have conversations on your Venmo transactions and treat the app like every other form of social media, set your transactions to private. I know employers, mainly current employees, search for candidates on every social media platform possible because I too have searched for a few people I have interviewed at previous companies. While bigger organizations will opt for a general background check service, smaller companies may do further due diligence. In fact, whoever is interviewing you may feel inclined to look at your LinkedIn, TikTok, and other social platforms to better help inform their decision. Some people research to gauge a candidate's professionalism in terms of social conduct, some may want to evaluate how the candidate will fit in with the company culture, and some may want to simply learn more about a candidate's qualifications.

By now you should understand why it's important to clean up your social media profiles. Take a moment to begin tidying yours. Do you start with Twitter, Facebook, Instagram, TikTok, or LinkedIn? The answer is you start with Google. Google yourself to find out what digital dirt you can uncover. Based on what you find, clean up as many incriminating photos and inappropriate status updates that you can find. No employer or graduate institution wants to see a pile of two-year-old tweets you have about your ex-girlfriend or boyfriend. They also don't want to see a bunch of tweets or Facebook statuses about how horrible your former boss was. It makes you look like an unpleasant person to work with. It may also lead to them asking further questions about the matter during your interview.

If you no longer use accounts that may have inappropriate data, delete them. There is no use in trying to manage accounts you no longer utilize. The first time I googled myself, I found a Google Plus account I created in 2009. The profile picture was me wearing a low-rise black chiffon skirt and a crop top displaying my belly ring while I was chucking up the peace sign and sticking my tongue out. The photo was taken in 2011, and back then it was cool to show your belly button ring. Not so much now, as I am in my twenties and such behavior is hard to justify as a working professional. I quickly closed the account and never looked back.

If you choose to keep unused accounts opened, set your profiles to be private. When I tell my friends or clients to delete certain photos, almost everyone questions why they need to. I know you may want to keep those pictures of you drinking a makeshift college cocktail out of a red solo cup, but I strongly advise you to download them to your desktop and delete every photo of you drinking or doing drugs. Yes, marijuana is still considered an illegal drug in some states. I know that deleting photos and content from your personal social media profiles is a time-consuming process, and you may consider it okay to keep public photos an employer may deem questionable. When you are going through your accounts, think of yourself as an employer or a CEO. Would you hire you with your current social media content? According to Career Savvy, one in three applicants are rejected simply because the employer found something online they did not like.

During an online survey, these were found to be the top four reasons candidates were rejected after being researched online:

- Inappropriate content posted
- Information about candidate drinking or using drugs
- Bad-mouthing previous employer
- Lied about qualifications

At this point, you should have googled yourself, deleted incriminating information, set profiles to private, and called any websites that have posted your information without your authorization. This entire process should not take you more than five hours, depending on the number of accounts you have.

The next step in spring cleaning, after researching and deleting, is updating. A picture is worth a thousand words, and that includes your profile picture. As I mentioned, unprofessional photos on your social pages should be removed, or the account should be set to private. The same rule applies to profile pictures. If you have an unprofessional or inappropriate profile picture, remove it. No one is saying all your profile pictures must be of you in a three-piece suit, but they should be quality and tasteful. These are the unspoken rules when it comes to profile pictures:

Default image	The default image for Twitter used to be an egg, and for many other social media platforms it is no more than a headshot silhouette. When you leave your profile picture on default, you come off as lazy and/or creepy. Think of all the friend requests you may have received and all the people you denied because they did not have a profile picture.
An image not of you	A random picture of an animal or a car can mess with your brand. Again, any profile picture that is not of you can sometimes come off as creepy.
Pixelated/ blurry image	Low-quality images are unprofessional.
Offensive image	A picture of your middle finger in the air or of something X-rated is *extremely* unprofessional and will come off as offensive and inappropriate.

There are many ways to look at cleaning up your social media. You can create three spheres as I have: one allowing for social freedom and no reigns, one allowing for integration between professional and personal, and one strictly and solely for professional purposes. The purpose of the social media clean-up is *not* to transform your entire social media life from structureless to rigidly complex. The purpose is to reevaluate your brand. How do you want to be seen in the world? A clean and presentable social media trace is far more beneficial than the opposite. If you want to post freely on Twitter, TikTok, Facebook, and Instagram and do not want to make a separate account, you should simply make sure each profile is private, or you run the risk of giving off the wrong impression. If you are into photography, modeling, or anything in the entertainment realm, you still want to clean up your social media to make sure what you want to represent is clear. The benefits of having tasteful social media profiles are unmatched.

During the same online survey mentioned earlier, these were found to be the top four reasons candidates were hired after being researched online:

- Good personality
- Presentable and professional profile image
- Wide range of interests
- Background information was accurate

Many employers and recruiters spend the same amount of time looking at your résumé and social media profiles. Employers spend an average of ten seconds looking at résumés and social profiles. Within this short time, they get what they need, which is why it is extremely important to make your profiles as presentable as possible. You only have ten seconds to impress and entice them to continue considering you for the position you applied for.

You have now googled yourself and removed anything that represents you in a less than pleasant way. You have deactivated useless accounts, contacted companies displaying your personal information, changed profile pictures, and set most of your accounts to private. The next thing you need to do is pay close attention to your LinkedIn. If you do not have a LinkedIn account, I need you to picture the great concern on my face. The level-ten, panicky kind of concern you have when your phone battery is at 1 percent and you have no charger; you're driving back home from a faraway place and you don't know where you are or how to read a map because you were born after 1990. If you have every other social media platform on the planet except a LinkedIn profile, you need to stop everything you are doing and create one. If you don't have a résumé in addition to not having a LinkedIn profile, my level of concern cannot even be pictured. Just know I am more concerned than a Nigerian parent after hearing their child has dropped out of school. After you make your LinkedIn account, you will need to create a résumé (more on this in Chapter 6) and then optimize from there. I have two categories of people when it comes to optimizing LinkedIn profiles: people with up-to-date résumés and people with outdated résumés. Depending on which category you fall into, the amount of time you will spend working on your profile will vary. Whether you belong in one category or the other, read the information on both.

LinkedIn for People with Up-to-Date Résumés

If you have an up-to-date résumé, optimizing your LinkedIn should take you no more than thirty minutes. You should transfer the majority of your resume to your LinkedIn profile; however, you should not list every task completed for each job. Instead list high-level achievements. Your LinkedIn is not meant to be a virtual CV. It should appear as a virtual synopsis of qualifications and professional experiences. Additionally, you want your experience as listed on both to match because any discrepancies may cause an employer to believe you are lying about your true qualifications. I interviewed a candidate for my former employer and followed up with my usual Google search. The first profile that popped up was their LinkedIn. Their résumé and LinkedIn were similar; however, the listed achievements on their résumé differed vastly from the achievements on their LinkedIn. I came to find out the candidate copied and pasted the job responsibilities listed by the company onto their résumé. During the interview, I asked the candidate to speak to the exact tasks they completed related to the job responsibilities for each role. For example: if the candidate listed on their résumé "developed a growth strategy focusing both on financial gain and customer satisfaction," I asked them to give the exact strategy they had developed in the past to allow for such an outcome.

The candidate could not fully explain because they did not *have* that experience; they wanted to ensure everything we were asking for was on paper. *Do not do this.* My employer, at the time, did not hire this candidate because they had falsified their qualifications. Your LinkedIn profile should highlight achievements, but do not list untrue things. The bottom line: fabricating your résumé or LinkedIn profile will only hurt you in the end. After looking over your LinkedIn profile, make sure it aligns with your résumé, and make sure your profile picture is presentable. Your picture *must* be professional. You should not have a picture of you in a swimsuit or with your friends.

LinkedIn for People with Outdated Résumés

If you have an outdated résumé, you should spend about an hour or two optimizing your LinkedIn profile. You will need to first update your résumé and then optimize your profile from there. If your outdated résumé lists jobs you held in high school, remove them, and do not put them on your LinkedIn profile. You are a semester or so away from receiving your bachelor's degree;

employers looking at your profile won't care that you worked at Domino's pizza in the eleventh grade.

Now that your social media life is in Career Savage order, you get to showcase your new and improved self. I challenge you to complete the Career Savage social media challenge. The Career Savage social media challenge will teach you the right way to use online platforms during your senior year and after that.

Career Savage Social Media Challenge
(make sure your social media profile is clean first)

Follow ten new accounts on Instagram, TikTok, and Twitter (ten each). These should be accounts of people within your career field (e.g., a music major would follow ten people in the music industry, or criminal justice major would follow ten people working in the criminal justice system).

For every picture you like on Instagram and for every video you like on TikTok, you should connect with someone new on LinkedIn. This requires you to pay close attention to your social media activity (e.g., if you like ten pictures while scrolling, you will now need to find ten new people to connect with on LinkedIn).

For every minute spent on Instagram, TikTok, or Twitter, you should spend half that time on LinkedIn looking for connections, applying to jobs, and messaging people in your career field (e.g., if you spent four hours on social media in one day, you would now need to spend at least two hours on LinkedIn).

For every comment you leave on someone's picture, reel, or video (Instagram or Tik Tok), you should send a direct message to someone in your career field (e.g., if you commented on two pictures and two videos in one day, you will now message four different people on one of the four social media platforms: Instagram, TikTok, Twitter, or LinkedIn).

Phase 3: Operation Build Your Network

You have finished the first two phases, and now it is time to move on to the big leagues. Throughout college, you might have heard the saying *your network is your net worth*. If for some reason you've never heard this, I would not be surprised. Again, this is why Career Savage was created to give you the information institutions have been neglecting to share. This saying is absolutely, totally, undoubtedly, the whole truth and nothing but the truth! I had to use all those extra buzzwords to get you to really understand that when you lack in your network, you lack in opportunities. Buzzwords are not enough to stress the importance of building a network. To get you to understand— and I mean *really* understand—how important a strong network is, I will explain how I got my first job, the importance of networking strategies, and the networking mistakes of my previous clients.

Building Bridges

I have two older brothers. My eldest brother, who is eight years older than me, is reserved and keeps a tight-knit circle. He chooses to have a network of only close friends and family. You could have known my brother for ten years and thought you were part of his circle, but realistically you know little about him. He isn't keen on acquaintances. Everyone he surrounds himself with is hand-selected, and he chooses to maintain those relationships for his intended purposes. As a result, he has people he can rely on and who would generally do anything for him. The genesis of his career derived from a long-standing friendship. Bottom line: his network is small, but the impact his network has is large. My next brother, on the other hand, is five years older than me and quite the opposite. He is outgoing and thrives best when his network is larger than life itself. His circle is vast, and because of this, he has someone in his network for *everything*. He is friends and/or acquaintances with musicians, celebrities, chemical engineers, and any other job title you can imagine.

Being the opportunist that I am, I inserted myself into both of my brothers' networks. The result? Many of my brothers' friends became my friends and, in turn, people in my network. I met one when I was eight years old. Let's call her Cristle. She is still in my life today, almost two decades later, and because of my relationship with her, I got my first corporate job at seventeen. I went from working as a special education tutor to an executive assistant. The experience I gained in that role kickstarted my career. I did not interview for the position, nor did I submit a résumé. The job was mine solely because Cristle was in my network, and she knew I was a capable individual. After working there for approximately a year, I extended the same gratitude to a former friend in my network. With my recommendation, she was hired without question—no résumé and no interview. The office staff was eventually made up of people in my and Cristle's network. When you have a strong network, you allow for many possibilities. My relationship with Cristle and the career opportunities it has presented are exactly why it is important to build your network and maintain it.

Burning Bridges

For this example, let's say my previous client's name is Jackson. Jackson was a college senior looking for a job like every other college graduate. Considering his network was rather small, he could not reach out to familial people for work opportunities and decided to blindly apply to a hundred or so places. He ended up contacting Career Savage and seeking consultation on the proper way to apply for jobs. I advised Jackson on what to do after reworking his résumé. Soon after, he messaged me and said my strategies resulted in many recruiters contacting him for various types of work (I'll explain the purpose of a recruiter in Chapter 6). After a few weeks, Jackson received a few job offers and decided to entertain two of them rather than going with one. Against my advisement, he committed to offer number one (farther commute, more money) while waiting to hear back from the other company, offer number two (closer in proximity but less money). *Now*, I advised Jackson to let the recruiter working on offer number one know he was waiting to hear back from another company and that he wanted to know if company one would give him more time to decide. He did not believe it was possible to ask for more time and assumed they would offer the position to another candidate. With this type of mindset, he decided to commit to offer number one.

I will pause for a moment to say that the last thing you want to do is screw over your recruiter and not be transparent. Recruiters truly and honestly work to get you the best possible offers. They also get job offers sent to them directly before they are posted online. This means a good relationship with recruiters gets you fast-track access to job opportunities. Two-timing your recruiter and treating them as if they are not your teammate is the quickest way to burn a bridge.

A week went by, and Jackson started at his new job, offer number one. On the same day, Jackson received a call confirming he got the job from company number two. He even leveraged an increase in salary to match company number one's offer. He accepted this job and did not show up for his first day of work at the first company. He called his recruiter for job offer number one to let them know he was rescinding his acceptance. The recruiter was extremely agitated, as I assumed they would be. The recruiter informed Jackson of his poor etiquette and that his actions are exactly how professional bridges get burned. I hated saying, "I told you so," but I told Jackson what the outcome would be beforehand. Despite the drama, Jackson is happy and still working for company number two; however, should he decide to move forward, he knows he can never contact that recruiter for help with another job opportunity.

The moral of these two stories is to build a strong network while working consciously not to destroy professionally beneficial relationships. Network with friends of friends and friends of family members. The larger your network, the greater the possibilities. When you have a large network, looking for jobs becomes a seamless process. You do not have to do much when your network is vast like my younger older brothers. If people in your network know you are on the job market, chances are they will reach out to you when opportunities become available.

I have worked within the regulatory affairs industry for a few years and can attest that the industry is only so big. Over the years, I had kept in touch with recruiters and colleagues so that when I was on the job market, I was the first person they thought to call. When I completed my master's degree, I knew I wanted a bigger and better opportunity, something mid-senior level that would challenge me cognitively. Before posting my résumé anywhere, I sent my updated CV/résumé to seven different recruiters. These were recruiters I formed close relationships with dating back to when I was a senior in college. I also sent my résumé to two talent acquisition representatives of contract research organizations I worked with through a previous employer. Of those nine people, all were thrilled to help me find another position. They sent every single regulatory, clinical, and clinical project management role to me before sending it to any other candidate. For a month, I was offered more jobs than I could count. I was living life while people were looking for jobs, *for me*! If these people were not in my network, this would not have been the case. I think you get the point of having a strong network by now.

You are a senior in college, and your network more likely than not includes your classmates and a few people you went to high school with. It is time to expand your horizons. Your network should be comprehensive and include people who know you well to acquaintances. If you are unsure where to look for people to add to your network, I recommend starting with LinkedIn. What's great about LinkedIn is that it makes connection suggestions for you, making networking even more seamless.

If you want to do more than scroll through LinkedIn, you will need to leave your campus and attend events related to the career you are interested in. Even if events surrounding your campus are unrelated to your career of interest, you should still attend. My network does not only have people in public health/medical professions. It is important to diversify your network, which is why I am connected with professionals from various industries. Take a night and skip going out to the bar with your friends to instead research networking events in your area. Meetup and Eventbrite offer many networking opportunities. Both have a lot to offer. The events posted on these platforms are not as stuffy as you are picturing them. It is not a whole bunch of people with briefcases standing around waiting to pass out their business cards. The settings, for the most part, are casual. During my junior year of college, I went home for one weekend. As every college student does when they return home, I made plans to meet up with my girlfriends. These girlfriends were three to five years older than me—I was twenty-one my junior year, and they were between twenty-four and twenty-six.

Do you remember Cristle? Well, Cristle and my other girlfriends invited me to a networking event at a popular LA rooftop bar. The networking event was for LA Market Week, also known as LA Fashion Market, the West Coast's premier fashion trade event. I love fashion, but my career surely is not based on it. Regardless, I decided to go and bask in the phenomenal LA night skyline. Upon arrival, we were each given two drink tickets and the freedom to roam and socialize. We did exactly that. The four of us each ended the night with useful contacts. Specific to my experience, I miraculously ended up speaking with a registered nurse for much of the night. She was there with a friend who owned a showroom in Los Angeles and decided to tag along. She shared useful career advice for Career Savage. I also ended up briefly speaking with a business owner who gave me advice I still follow today, as it relates to running Career Savage.

Do you see how an event unrelated to my career still resulted in receiving information applicable to my career passions and life? It was a fun night filled with opportunities to connect with like-minded people. When you attend networking events like this, come ready to socialize and speak on your career passions and interests.

You now know you need to build your network and have an idea of where to start. In addition to networking events on

Meetup and Eventbrite, career fairs are the more traditional route to building your professional network and finding a job. You need to know what to expect when attending such events. Career fairs are considered some of the best places to network for soon-to-be college graduates. Your college or university should have career fairs throughout the year; these tend to pick up in frequency the closer it gets to graduation day. If for some reason your college or university does not host career fairs, you can check www.NationalCareerFairs.com to see where and when the closest career fair is, or if there are any virtual fairs on www.joinhandshake.com. You can also check if schools surrounding yours are hosting any. Some schools may check your student ID before entering the fair, so you will need to confirm if students from other schools can attend.

Going to a career fair is not like the rooftop networking event I mentioned above. It's not cocktails and conversations; it is essentially a pre-pre-interview with employers. You come dressed in business attire with your résumé in hand. You are there to talk to potential employers about your career and job openings that best suit your interests. You should feel comfortable discussing any work experience you have. I compare career fairs to speed dating. You go from booth to booth discussing what you have to offer and what the company offers in return. To make the "interview" process at a career fair easy, be personable and know your pitch. A key part of effective networking is being clear about your employment expectations and career goals. Prepare talking points and practice delivering them. Be able to speak confidently about what you want and what you have to offer.

The first career fair I attended, I made sure I could speak about pharmaceuticals and my pursuit in medicine with ease. I eloquently spoke upon my pharmacy technician experience and how I wanted to translate that into a more impactful healthcare career (more on this outcome in Chapter 6). Before you leave, make sure to collect business cards. Some booths will run out of business cards; in that case, collect emails and phone numbers. When the day is done and you have successfully connected with employers, send an email or LinkedIn message the next day thanking the company representative for their time. After a few weeks, if you have not heard anything from the people who said they had a job that matched your qualifications, follow up with them. Remember, the general Career Savage rule of thumb is to reach out three times, then let it be.

Career Savage Career Fair Checklist
(check off completed tasks)

_____ Find a career fair to attend.

_____ Find a business outfit to wear.

_____ Update résumé (especially contact information).

_____ Print twenty copies of résumé. (A résumé should be one page. It can be two pages printed as one double-sided page. Have a folder to prevent the résumés from becoming crinkled.)

_____ Practice your pitch.

_____ Collect employer contact information.

_____ Follow up with employers one day after.

_____ Follow up with employers periodically.

Phase 4: Perhaps, Graduate School

Often, students mistakenly begin to think about law school, medical school, and graduate school during the first semester of senior year. I hate to be the one to say this, but if you plan to pursue a postgraduate education immediately after undergrad, you should have started the process your sophomore/junior year of college. There are exams (e.g., MCAT and LSAT) you must take before applying that require rigorous preparation. I was sporadic with my medical school application process (more on this in Chapter 3). I did not know what I was doing, nor did I prepare any real timelines, which resulted in my gap year.

For seniors interested in attending graduate school, there is still hope if you just began to think about it this semester. Although you should have begun preparing your application during your junior year, there is more leeway with the graduate school application process compared to the medical and law school application process. You will need to be strategic because most graduate school deadlines fall from October 1 to December 31. While I do not recommend rushing through any academic application process and advise you apply the next cycle, if you do decide to apply, these are the things you need to do before the end of December:

- Look into schools you want to apply to and their deadlines
- Study for and take the GRE
- Gather letters of recommendation
- Write your personal statement
- Have your personal statement peer reviewed
- Complete actual application

Once you've completed those tasks, you can then submit your application to the schools of your choice. As you can see, a lot needs to be completed, and you are only giving yourself approximately thirty days to do everything. The best-case scenario is a school's deadline is January 1, giving you extra days to complete the listed tasks.

I empower everyone I cross paths with to challenge themselves educationally, but this strict timeline may not give you the time you need to prepare the best possible application. Do not force yourself to apply to graduate school because you feel there is nothing else for you to do after graduation or because it is the safest bet. In reality, you may be wasting your money going back to school to get a degree you are not 100 percent sure you want. There is much for you after graduation. Especially if you use Career Savage strategies to get you what your heart desires! The intended purpose of getting a master's or doctorate is because you are absolutely certain of the profession you want to remain in. Don't be the person who gets a master's in environmental science and ends up working as a product manager for a software company.

During the first semester, a lot of things need to be accomplished. Vibing and raging sounds fun until you are a college graduate wondering how it's possible to have a bachelor's and be working in a warehouse lifting boxes. As I mentioned at the start of this guide, you may feel tempted to attend everything you're invited to. You may start to think about being separated from your friends come graduation, and you will want to spend every moment with them while you still can. That or you may have serious FOMO (fear of missing out) and make the mistake of focusing on things that won't matter when you graduate. In reality, time will not stop once graduation day comes. Corporations and other organizations do not follow a college/

university schedule, and career opportunities will be pulled from underneath you. I went to parties in moderation, and I advise you do the same. Assuming you already have a job related to your major or are now frantically looking for one, here are all the tasks you should complete during your final first semester of college (check off completed tasks):

Check Off Completed Tasks:

_____ Create an appropriate email account solely for applying to jobs (i.e., sallysavage@gmail.com).

_____ For every thirty minutes spent on Instagram, TikTok, and Twitter, spend half that time on LinkedIn.

_____ Attend at least one career fair or career-networking event per month.

_____ Have a career coach/strategist (e.g., Career Savage) look over your résumé.

_____ Build your network.

_____ Clean up your social media profiles.

_____ Have a friend take a professional profile picture for you.

_____ Reconnect with people from your summer internship, *if applicable.*

_____ Work on graduate school applications.

You don't have to be as boring as I was—drinking a glass of Apothic red wine on weekends while binge-watching *Grey's Anatomy* and scrolling through job postings on Indeed—but make sure you don't get sucked into a vortex where you think you have all the time in the world to prepare for graduation. You have a lot to do senior year in addition to attending classes and hopefully working. You should be preparing for the future.

CHAPTER 4

Winter Break

"When patterns are changed, new worlds emerge."
—TULI KUPFERBERG

Winter can only mean one thing. After finals week, you get a month-long break from exams, group projects, and assignments. Your approach to winter break in the past may have consisted of solely hanging with friends and celebrating the winter season, but this time around, your approach should be different. Each break during your senior year should be approached the same way I advised you to approach the summer: with your end goal in mind. While you may be tired from the semester and in need of a break, think forwardly. I want you to pause here and ask yourself if you would prefer to use this winter break as an opportunity to look for jobs, intern, and/or work or if you would prefer to use this time as a much-needed vacation.

'Tis the Season to Be Working

No one truly enjoys working during the holidays. They'd much rather be with family, opening presents, eating home-cooked meals, and toasting to a great year ahead. I spent my Christmas Eve, Christmas Day, and New Year's Eve holidays talking to my pharmacist about titrating patients' blood with sodium bicarbonate and running medications up to the ICU. I would have enjoyed spending those holidays with my family, but I chose to sacrifice for the sake of continuing to gain experience while in school. My choice was an act of delayed gratification. After graduating and entering corporate America, I never worked a holiday, including my birthday.

One winter season, I even spent five days in New York, followed by ten days in Portugal, and then five days in Dubai. Every sacrifice I made senior year resulted in the fortunate lifestyle I could live as a postgraduate. If I had chosen instant gratification, I would have spent the entire winter break in New York with my extended family, partying at Hudson Yard, shopping in SoHo, and hanging out with friends at every bar south of Harlem. This decision would have cost me career experiences that ultimately helped me find a job at the end of graduation and admittance into a graduate program one year after graduating. How I decided to spend my winter break senior year afforded me the privilege of strengthening my biochemistry knowledge, which resulted in my overall MCAT score improving. I also had the flexibility to focus on building core relationships with recruiters in my field.

You may think it's ridiculous to spend every waking moment during winter break thinking about your future, and I agree. I would be lying to you if I said I didn't have a moment to myself or a moment to enjoy the holiday break. I enjoyed my breaks with some balance. Most of the time, I was either working, studying, or looking for a job. However, I did get the chance to have restful sleep and hang out with friends who lived in Connecticut. To my surprise, I spent a lot of time outside of work with my coworkers. I normally refrain from getting too close to people I work with, but my hospital friends were different. Let's refer to them as Nate and Monica. Both were kindergarten best friends who worked as waiters for the hospital kitchen. We were the only staff in our early twenties, so we naturally gravitated toward each other. Monica always tried to get me to go out with them, and one night, at the beginning of winter break, I said yes.

"Where are we going?" I asked.

Nate turned around, smirked, and said, "A rodeo."

"Shut up. We are not going to a rodeo." Monica laughed.

"Okay, we are going to a bar that has a mechanical bull," Nate replied.

"Oh wow! I've never ridden a mechanical bull before," I said with excitement.

They looked at each other with a smile and responded, "We figured."

"You're always working or studying, so it's unlikely you've ventured through Connecticut."

Nate's remark didn't bother me. People made comments like that all the time, and I always knew that my laser focus would only result in a better life and career.

We arrived at the bar and spent hours dancing, laughing, and enjoying each other's company. The excitement of the night made me realize that, at times, my rigid schedules had kept me from experiencing happy moments. I knew the sacrifices I was making were for the greater good, but a healthy balance would be just as effective. From that one night on, I altered my perception. I continued to work and study but decided to give myself one day off a week. A day I was free to use at my discretion.

Earlier, I asked how you would like to spend your winter break: developing or partying? Whatever you choose to do, the one thing you should do is set winter goals. If you have a job, working through the winter season, it will take up a lot of your time. You may have fewer goals on your list as a result of that. If you opt not to work or intern, your goals should be robust to help prevent a loss of motivation. Sitting around your parents' house for four to five weeks sounds amazing, but it can also kickstart senioritis (more on this in Chapter 5). I want you to take some time to prepare for winter break and set some goals for yourself similar to the goals I set for myself at the time. If there were ventures you never completed during the summer, now would be the time to complete those.

Kyyah's Winter Break Savage Plan of Action

Complete the Action(s)	My Savage Plan
Start studying for the MCAT	Purchase the new *Kaplan 528 MCAT Advanced Prep* workbook and use this as a blueprint for studying. Study two hours before and during each shift. Study one hour after shift. Study eight hours on on-workdays.
Work with an MCAT tutor	Have the pharmacist at work act as my tutor. He was a biochemist and could help with biochemistry (my weakest subject). Request to work every night he works. Nights are slower and allow for more tutor time. Have the pharmacist explain the mechanism of action for every medication I deliver and every IV I make.
Apply to jobs: • Upload résumé to job boards • Network on LinkedIn • Apply to ten jobs everyday	Turn on "open to new opportunities" feature on LinkedIn. Upload résumé to CareerBuilder, Indeed, Monster, ZipRecruiter, and Glassdoor. Network on LinkedIn when en-route to work and home. Apply to jobs recommended on Indeed before going to bed each evening.

My Winter Break Savage Plan of Action

Complete the Action(s)	My Savage Plan

The Prepared Graduate

I used to hate the saying, "Hindsight is twenty-twenty," but it truly is. An idle winter break can easily lead to a lack of motivation, which happened to a lot of my friends. They returned to school from winter break and didn't care to prepare for classes, let alone graduation. In speaking with some of them presently, they all wished they took their last months leading up to graduation a little more seriously. Most are still learning to navigate their careers and are just beginning to learn what I am sharing with you in this book. You may think looking for jobs six months before graduation is excessive, but for new graduates, the application process can be long. The longest job application process I ever experienced was seven months. As highlighted in my example, your winter break doesn't require a militant schedule centered on career development. Breaks are pivotal for success. As winter breaks are meant for spending time with the people you love, you should do that while working on necessary tasks that will benefit your advancements. Even if you can only make one connection on LinkedIn every few days, the right connection could result in a job opportunity.

Professional Degrees Don't Happen Overnight

Outside of experiences, winter break brought many realizations. I was so wrapped up in the craziness of college that I paid no attention to the timelines of medical school matriculation. Considering I mentioned medical school to my advisor several times, I foolishly assumed they would remind me when to begin the application process. Additionally, my summer internship made me question going to medical school altogether. A few weeks before winter break, I was outlining goals for myself and included taking the MCAT. As I dissected the application process further, I realized I was behind the AAMC-advised timeline. As a senior, I had just begun preparing for the MCAT while others were preparing for their interviews. This is the timeline I should have followed if I wanted to matriculate the fall succeeding spring graduation:

Medical School Timeline

January to December (sophomore year)	Study for and take the MCAT. Do other preparatory work.
January (junior year)	Complete a list of schools.
January to March (junior year)	Write personal statement.
May (junior year)	Submit AMCAS primary application.
July (junior year)	Submit AMCAS secondary applications.
September to April (senior year)	Interview season.
May (senior year)	Confirm and commit to a medical school. Waitlists will move significantly in May as students commit to schools.
June to August (post-graduation)	Celebrate on getting into school.
Fall immediately after graduating college	Medical school starts.

I was aiming in so many directions I ended up missing my number one target: medical school. I felt blindsided in realizing I couldn't attend in the fall, and at the same time realized hadn't focused on getting an acceptance. I focused on gaining experience to secure a job opportunity.

This winter, take time and ask yourself if graduate school or a doctoral program is something you desire. If you are unsure of the timelines for acceptance, make it a goal to curate a plan. There is a lot of advice around finding job opportunities in this book, but understanding whether or not more school is in your plans is just as important.

While most doctoral timelines span out two to three years, some graduate program applications can be completed during your senior year. For example, MBA programs have three application cycles. Round 1 deadlines are in September/October, round 2 deadlines are in January, and round 3 deadlines are in March/April. This means, if you desire to get your MBA, you can submit your application in April at the latest for matriculation in the summer/fall. However, you should consider that some business programs want you to have a few years of relevant work experience before applying. It's the number one criterion for competitive applicants, but requirements will vary for each school. I can assure you the top twenty business schools in the country require applicants to have professional work experience. If you are rushing to apply during your senior year simply to meet the deadline, you may submit it on time, but you may not receive an acceptance with such a subpar application.

In taking some time to think about your future and completing the winter goals you set for yourself, you'll be well prepared to navigate your second semester. As I previously noted, the purpose of giving yourself tasks to complete while on break is to one, not fall victim to senioritis early, and two, to start thinking about life after graduation. Take a moment to incorporate your goals into your winter break schedule.

EXAMPLE						
MONDAY	TUESDAY	WEDNESDAY	THURSDAY	FRIDAY	SATURDAY	SUNDAY
Apply to five jobs	Work on personal statements for medical school	Study for MCAT	Take MCAT practice test	Network with five recruiters	Apply to five jobs	BREAK

Week 1						
MONDAY	TUESDAY	WEDNESDAY	THURSDAY	FRIDAY	SATURDAY	SUNDAY
						BREAK

Week 2						
MONDAY	TUESDAY	WEDNESDAY	THURSDAY	FRIDAY	SATURDAY	SUNDAY
						BREAK

Week 3						
MONDAY	TUESDAY	WEDNESDAY	THURSDAY	FRIDAY	SATURDAY	SUNDAY
						BREAK

Week 4						
MONDAY	TUESDAY	WEDNESDAY	THURSDAY	FRIDAY	SATURDAY	SUNDAY
						BREAK

Week 5						
MONDAY	TUESDAY	WEDNESDAY	THURSDAY	FRIDAY	SATURDAY	SUNDAY
						BREAK

CHAPTER 5

Second Semester

"If you're going through hell, keep going."
—WINSTON CHURCHILL

While I knew being eighteen in high school came with an influx of cool new privileges, I truly cared for only a few. Sure, I could purchase lottery tickets and drive without an adult being in the car, but the greatest privilege was signing myself out of school without my mother ever knowing. I managed to miss more than fifty track practices and thirty choir rehearsals. I would attend my core courses from 7:00 a.m. to 11:00 a.m. and then head home for my daily dose of Meredith Grey and Christina Yang. My mother will officially find out when she chooses to read this book. I knew I needed to maintain a B average to forgo the possibility of losing my college acceptance and scholarships, but senioritis had a hold on me. It was an odd experience. I lost all motivation, inspiration, and desire to do anything related to academia. There were days I would sign myself out of class and go home to garden. Yes, garden. It became a routine to pull into my driveway at noon, walk straight from the front door to my backyard, and put on gloves to begin planting rose bushes and lemon trees. My friends would ask me why I skipped so many classes, and I would tell them: "I'm growing a garden." They thought I was kidding until one day, my friend followed me home from school. She saw me pull into the driveway, walk to my backyard, and put on gardening gloves.

"Oh, you were serious," she said from a distance.

Startled, I asked, "What are you doing here?"

"We're worried about you. You're acting really weird, and suddenly you're just never at school," my friend said with concern.

"Yeah, because I don't care." I laughed. "In two months, you'll be in North Carolina, and I'll be Connecticut. We all have our acceptances, so I don't see the point in stressing myself out by going to class every day."

"You still have to pass all your classes," she reminded me.

"And I will," I responded confidently.

I continued to garden as my friend said her goodbyes and left to return to school. Senioritis is hard to explain. You've spent almost four years working toward your degree and for some reason, you hit a wall before crossing the finish line. As I experienced senioritis in high school, I was withdrawn and truly desired to close one chapter in order to move on to the next one in my life: college.

Triple S: Second Semester Senioritis

I graduated from high school and embarked on my journey to college, thinking the senioritis experience was exclusive to high school. To my surprise, I experienced the same feelings the second semester of my senior year in college. I recognized all the senioritis symptoms early: binge-watching *Grey's Anatomy*, frequently skipping class, and avoiding people I knew because I wore the same tracksuit and Uggs for four days in a row. This sounds a lot like depression, but I promise you, it was nothing more than a classic case of senioritis. If you do feel your senioritis may be creeping toward depression, I strongly suggest you talk to a psychologist on campus, your friends, or your family. Everyone's senioritis symptoms will be different, but many seniors may experience:

- Low energy (me)
- Low motivation (me)
- Frequent naps (me)
- General confusion
- Overwhelming misery
- Poor personal hygiene (guilty: don't judge)
- Severe procrastination (me)
- Excessive daydreaming (me)
- Total indifference about education and working (me)
- Diminished ability to concentrate
- Lack of concern about upcoming exams and assignments (also me)
- Sloppy, out-of-character fashion choices (me, again)

Before you go around analyzing the differences in how senioritis and depression manifests in you and your friends, I must say this list is not meant to be used in lieu of seeing a licensed clinical professional.

Senioritis has the potential to derail you from meeting your career objectives. Unlike my high school graduation, I had no job offers and no real plan, so I tried hard to fight the temptations of slacking off. I did everything from giving myself tasks to complete over winter break (refer to Chapter 4) to taking on more shifts at the hospital. I would skip a lecture to watch *Grey's Anatomy* only to be disappointed in myself and show up to every class early the following week. While I felt that exhaustion was directly causing my sluggish demeanor, I still tried to fight anything that could worsen my senioritis.

I persistently fought off the lack of motivation by actively applying to jobs. The résumés I posted on job boards during winter break were taken down every two weeks and re-uploaded to keep my résumé at the top of recruiters' search lists. I was blindly applying to every job I could find in addition to networking with colleagues and recruiters. I tried to leverage a promotion from the hospital but no openings piqued my interest. There was a microbiology lab assistant position open, but it did not require a bachelor's degree. I wanted my degree to signify something. I felt as if it had to. Those long nights in the library, horrific organic chemistry exams, and nights screaming into my pillow from the stress of being a college student meant I was going to get a job that required a four-year degree.

I could have remained a pharmacy technician, but I thought, *Do you want to graduate from college just to work the same job you were eligible to work while in college?* Many students do this, and there is nothing wrong with this *if* it's your only option. Many tell themselves, worst-case scenario, "I will just work the job I have now after graduating from school." Do not incorporate stagnancy into your development plans. It can only fuel your senioritis. Manifestation is cliché, but it's a cliché with great significance. You are mentally setting yourself up to settle. Tell yourself you will not remain where you are after working so hard to claim your degree. This will give you more motivation and confidence to find the job you deserve.

Who, What, When, and Where to Apply

While I was applying to jobs, I had no direction, no advice, no guidance, nothing. When I went to my advisor asking what possible jobs I could apply to as a pre-med biology major, there was a subtle blank stare in his eyes. He was unable to help me in the way I needed. I have always wondered why advisors don't give their students a list of jobs to investigate at the start of their college careers. How else are students supposed to know what's out there and what their options are? Every major has a generic career path, but options should be detailed and talked through with students. Not every criminal justice major wants to be a criminologist, and not every biology major wants to go to medical school or work in a lab. I was shocked to learn of all the other career opportunities available to science majors. If students are made aware of their options on day one, it would give them a greater chance of excelling post-graduation. There would also be less confusion on how to navigate your career.

Nonetheless, I did not know what I was doing while applying, and you may feel the same way. Luckily you have Career Savage strategies underway to make the process a little easier.

The number one question clients ask me is, "How did you know what jobs to apply for?" Everything I am telling you to do in preparation for graduation is intended to help you get a job and decide what you want to do. The relevant experience you should be gaining while attending school is meant to help you decide. I went from a retail pharmacy to a clinical pharmacy because I realized interfacing with patients and insurers is not something I enjoy. In having that experience, I was one step closer to figuring out what I wanted to do. I once desired to be a pediatrician. After volunteering in a pediatric oncology unit, I realized I could never be an oncologist, nor could I ever directly work with seriously ill pediatric patients. The job requires a certain type of spirit to hold such a position.

Posting your résumé on job platforms and tagging them with words related to your major and career interests is supposed to help you decide as well. After I posted my résumé and tagged "biology," "pharmaceutical," and "medical," I got calls for clinical affairs, regulatory affairs, medical sales, and, of course, pharmacy technician jobs. All these calls helped me better understand what roles are available to people who possess a biology degree. That said, these were the types of roles I sought out and applied for:

- Regulatory affairs assistant
- Regulatory affairs associate
- Regulatory affairs specialist
- Research assistant
- Pharmaceutical biologist
- Chemist
- Biologist
- Medical affairs associate
- Clinical research associate
- Clinical trial associate
- Associate clinical research project manager

- Clinical research project coordinator
- Clinical research coordinator

I applied to 627 jobs by the time early May rolled around. You may wonder how I managed to apply to all these jobs while working, going to class, and maintaining a social life. I had to practice a new level of discipline I had never practiced before. If you apply to six jobs a day throughout your semester, you will surpass my ambitious number of applications. With platforms like LinkedIn adding new features, applying for jobs has truly become seamless. If you turn on the "open to new opportunities" feature, you will witness opportunities coming to you. Of the 627 jobs I applied to, I received nearly the same number of rejections in addition to no response from the remaining organizations. The lack of opportunities only worsened my anxiety. As you apply for jobs, you may experience the same issues I encountered. In hindsight, I can tell you what I wished I knew to make applying for jobs an easier process. The number one thing I wish I had done was spend more time networking at in-person events. If I had focused more on building my network than blindly applying, I might have procured an opportunity sooner than I did. Throughout this entire text, I will continue to stress the importance of having a strong network of working professionals in your field. From this day until the day you retire, understand that your network will always bring you the most opportunities. You've now been talked through the signs of senioritis and the importance of applying for jobs second semester. Beyond this, there is general advice I wish I received venturing into the second semester of my senior year.

Battling Through Second Semester

Everyone advises college freshmen before they enter their first year of college, but where do all these people go when it's time to advise college seniors? It's scary how alone and uneasy seniors feel entering their last year of college. From emotional to physical stress, seniors singlehandedly are the most misguided group of college students. People who are meant to matriculate into the workforce after college graduation should feel sure (instead of completely unsure) of where their life is headed. Of course, it is the result of not receiving real career guidance. Fortunately, Career Savage has five notable points seniors should follow.

Don't Procrastinate

If you do procrastinate, at least manage to complete *and pass* your classes. Procrastination is the most common reason students get bad grades. You get invited to a party, stay out all night, go to McDonald's at 4:00 a.m. because you're anything but sober, sleep until noon, and before you know it, your twenty-page paper is due in twelve hours and you haven't even looked at the book you are supposed to write about. While the best advice I could give you is to *simply not* procrastinate in the first place, if you do, just get back on track and fast. Procrastination is the thief of time, and essentially, you are only robbing yourself. If you must pull an all-nighter to study for your midterm or finish your research paper, suck it up and just do it. Grab some coffee or a Red Bull, go to the library, and stay there until your uncompleted assignments get done. Don't let the combination of senioritis and procrastination keep you from *actually graduating*. Many fifth-year seniors on campus can attest to not passing one or two classes their senior year.

"Passing" a class has many definitions. At some universities, a D is passing, but by Career Savage standards, a C is passing. By now, we know GPAs don't matter for every major, but don't turn in poor work and accept a D in every class just for the sake of it. You may want to go to graduate school later, and the poor grades you earned at the end of your undergraduate career will ultimately come back and negatively affect you. I highly doubt all Ds are considered "passing" at any university, but all Ds results in a 1.00 GPA (see GPA chart below). Even just a few Ds in one semester can exponentially drop the GPA you worked so hard to maintain all four years. Yes, I did get some Ds during my college career, and yes, I did have to make up for those Ds later. To figure out how your GPA will be affected by a poor semester, visit gpacalculator.net. This way, you can understand how a poor grade may affect you ahead of time.

Grade Point Average Chart

Grade	Grade Point Equivalent
A	4.00
A-	3.67
B+	3.33
B	3.00
B-	2.67
C+	2.33
C	2.00
D	1.00
F	0.00

Start Planning Your Next Steps Now

Throughout this entire guide, the concepts of planning and foresight have been consistently discussed. By now, you should understand that by the second semester of senior year, your planning should be in overdrive. You don't have to be a type-A perfectionist with your planning, but you should be familiar with your career field and areas of interest. If you aren't, start researching what types of jobs you can get with your degree.

You need to start looking for what you are going to do after you graduate. Begin polishing your résumé, start applying for jobs, initiate practicing your interview skills, and continue networking. Again, I have already mentioned much of this throughout the book, but I am repeating myself to stress the importance of planning your next steps. You can do all of this on your own or contact Career Savage for help with the process.

Get Organized

Freshman year, your agenda was most likely in pristine condition. You wrote down everything, from assignments to dentist appointments. You also, more likely than not, kept your dorm room neat and tidy. As the years went on, you cared less and less about your agenda and your room. Now is the time to get back to caring. Senior year is your busiest year yet, and organization will certainly help you excel. Organize files on your computer to minimize headaches while applying for jobs and completing homework assignments. Set reminders on your phone so you don't miss deadlines and clean your room. Someone once told me a messy room equates to a messy life, and I have to agree.

Network

I have said it before, and I will say it again: network. One thing I want you to remember while networking is to allow for an organic connection. There is nothing worse than an opportunistic pushy person. Whether you are networking with peers, professors, mentors, or potential employers, don't force the connection. Engage in an organic conversation, exchange contact information when you meet someone of interest, and carry on. If you do choose to follow up with the person, they will remember you as not pushy and be more inclined to engage with you further.

Be Careful of Getting into a Relationship

You may think this is completely unrelated to a successful senior year and finding a job after college, but I am here to politely tell you, you are mistaken. If you have been in a relationship for the majority of college and you have made it to senior year stronger than ever, this likely won't apply to you. For seniors who begin a relationship during senior year, you are setting yourself up. Hear me out. Many of the Career Savage strategies you have now implemented or will implement will provide you with opportunities across the nation. Right now, you may be going to school in New York, but come graduation, you may get offered a full-time job with benefits in Los Angeles. With your partner also figuring out their career plans, what do you do? Do you stay in New York to save your relationship, or do you take the job? The answer depends on the kind of person you are and how important your career is to you. I almost turned down a job that launched my career because of a temporary relationship. Ultimately, you should make the best decision for yourself and your life.

Of all the advice you have received for the second semester, the additional advice I am about to give will be the most important. At the start of the new semester, you should begin to mentally prepare yourself for the new world you will step into to prevent sudden shock. After graduating, many things will change.

My roommate Noelle and I were the only two people within our friend group to graduate on time. We both moved out of our house and into our separate new spaces in New Haven, while the rest of our friends remained close to campus to complete their graduation requirements. The shift from waking up to my best friends every morning and hanging out in the dining hall on campus to waking up for my nine-to-five almost put me in a depressive state. When I left Connecticut for Los Angeles, my sadness worsened, knowing I was now across the country, away from my friends, in an environment I was required to relearn. College is unlike anything else. It's almost like being away at camp for four years. You laugh, cry, and enjoy pivotal moments in your life with people who grow to become your family. Part of preparing for life after college is enjoying these last moments with your friends. Your career is important. Looking for a job and ensuring you graduate into a moderately stable life is important too. However, these are moments you will *never* get back. I sometimes wish I could repeat years of my college experience just to laugh with my roommates or sarcastically joke around with my friends in the quad one more time. You can prepare for life after college and still enjoy moments with your college family. It's all about balance.

CHAPTER 6

A Not-So-Savage Spring Break

"I'm not here for a long time; I'm here for a good time."
—SPRING BREAKERS DURING THE COVID-19 PANDEMIC

College spring break, another "last" to add to your list. Most seniors will choose to spend their last break making memories they want to forget and spending money they don't have in a typical spring break hotspot. Regardless, most students who decide to vacation as opposed to preparing for reality will come back to school far more stressed than when they left. Why? Because they thought spring break was the solution to their graduation anxiety.

Don't let my cynicism fool you: I love spring break season. I enjoy the blooming of alstroemerias and hydrangeas following the April showers and the start of BBQs and other sunny outdoor gatherings. I love how perfectly balanced the weather is just about everywhere, but I know you don't care about my feelings on weather and picnics in the park. You want to know how you should spend your spring break.

As you read this, you are likely exploring all spring break possibilities. You don't want to miss out on any fun. Before you decide, you should consider a few things. First, stop thinking this is your last spring break. You're not leaving earth. You're just leaving college. After you graduate into the real world, you can take a vacation whenever you want. That is why most jobs offer something magical called *paid time off*. If you want to remain on a college schedule, you can always opt to take a vacation when colleges go on break. Why would you want to do this? I haven't a clue, but I do know people who have done it. They schedule their work vacation when their younger friends are on break or when they know typical spring break locations will be active. It helped them ease into the schedule differences between college life and real life.

Springing Into No Offers

A few weeks before break, you may still be experiencing graduation anxiety, which directly leads to fear you will graduate with no job and no direction. Considering graduation is no more than two and a half months away, you may also constantly be thinking about your student loans and how you can afford to pay them back. You may start to imagine moving back into your parents' home and following the rules you once had to at eighteen. You may begin to spiral and wonder, "What am I going to do?"

If it provides you with any sense of comfort, you are not alone. Just about every senior asks themselves these questions and worries at least a little. Even the ones who appear to have it all together are scared too. Life after college is different, and the thought of adjusting and leaving a space you were comfortable in for four or more years causes any normal person to feel apprehensive.

Weeks before spring break, I asked myself the same questions and ended up having a panic attack. There was a hollowness in my stomach, a thrashing of my heart, and an unsteadiness in my hands. I dropped one knee to the floor, and the other followed. I placed my hands down and fell into a fetal position. As I laid on the floor and let my anxieties soak into my cocoa brown carpet, my eyes filled with tears. I didn't know what to do. At that moment, I felt helpless. For the fearless girl who moved halfway across the country to attend school in an unfamiliar state, I was nervous about the future. After thirty minutes of mindless thinking, I did the only thing I thought would help alleviate my anxieties. I called my cousin.

For this story, let's call her Tiwa. She graduated from Emory University two years prior, and to my surprise, she told me she had a similar experience. While her experience may not have been as severe as mine, she too was unsure where she would work leading up to graduation but trusted everything would work out the way it was supposed to, and it did. She applied to jobs vigorously throughout her final months in college and leveraged her internships to get a job. She went on to work for one of the largest investment management firms in the nation. As I expected though, listening to her experiences only helped at that moment. I still had a million and one questions for myself. If this isn't you, great—you have mastered the art of not worrying about what you cannot control. You have implemented Career Savage strategies, and you are waiting for your hard work to present itself in the form of a job offer. But if this is you, it doesn't have to be.

I am not here to tell you not to enjoy any of your breaks. Ultimately, you will do as you wish. I suggest having balance during this spring break, which is something I failed at doing.

Make the Right Choice for *You*

A week before spring break, my best friend planned to go home and asked if I wanted to join. Not everyone has a best friend who lives in the Bahamas. Many were surprised when I turned down the offer. Reflecting on that moment, I wish I had booked my ticket and jetted off to paradise. I spent a good amount of time punishing myself because I had not yet landed a job. Again, do not do this. I should have enjoyed my spring break while also doing small tasks that would have helped me land a job come graduation. Although I am advising you to enjoy your break, you should still perform some important tasks. Doing some small tasks allows you to enjoy your well-deserved time off while staying ahead on the job-search front. To keep things light and stress-free, complete the list below every day during this break:

Spring Break To-Do List:
- Email university faculty or alumni in your career field of interest asking for advice on places to apply for work and/ or ask for a job referral.
- Apply to a minimum of two jobs on Indeed or LinkedIn.
- Connect with someone on LinkedIn in your career field of interest (attach a message with each connection request).

The list is simple enough. You can complete the entire thing in less than an hour. Use the following email template when reaching out to faculty:

Dear [*Insert title and name here*],

I hope this email finds you well. As you may know, I will be graduating this [insert season] with my bachelor's in [*insert degree here*]. I have decided to pursue employment in the [insert career field] industry and felt you were the best person to ask for career advice and job-seeking guidance. I have been networking with professionals who work in the [*insert career field*] industry and proactively applying for jobs. I plan to keep at this until I receive an offer and attend career fairs once we return from spring break. I wanted to ask if you know of anyone looking to hire new graduates in the [*insert career field*] industry or if you know of specific job titles I should be searching for. Here are the following positions I have already investigated:

• [List the position titles]

Lastly, if you have any general career advice you think I should know, I would truly enjoy hearing your perspective. I hope to hear from you soon. Enjoy the remainder of your break!

Kind regards,

[*Insert your signature here*]

Use the following message template when connecting with people on LinkedIn:

> Hello!
>
> My name is [*insert name here*] and I am an upcoming graduate from the [*insert university/college name here*]. I am graduating with my bachelor's in [*insert degree here*] this [*insert season here*] and have been reaching out to professionals in the industry I hope to work in. I would enjoy hearing your insight if you have any general career advice for employment with [insert company name]. Hope to hear from you.
>
> All the best,
>
> [*insert your name here*]

Don't feel uncomfortable reaching out to people in your field on LinkedIn. The worst that could happen is they don't answer, but more times than not, people respond. You have to remember they were once college students too. LinkedIn is a powerful tool, and Millennials and Gen Z'ers fail to use it as frequently as they should. When you message someone from your field on LinkedIn, the outcomes are endless. A simple message could lead you to the job you want. While the template above is useable in most cases, feel inclined to tweak the structure to best suit your needs. If you prefer to ask how to get a certain position or what questions may be asked for a role you are interviewing for, modify the template to include these components. Always remember you have a better chance of getting the job you want through your network than by blindly applying. LinkedIn is a realm where most professionals simply want to help other professionals.

Now, why am I suggesting you do spend spring break differently than I did? I did not stay up late going out. I didn't hang out with friends at the beach. I worked, studied, connected with recruiters, and applied to as many jobs as I could per day. By now, you should be familiar with the importance of working a major-relevant job while in school, finishing strong, not failing because of senioritis, and proactively applying to jobs. The issue with my strategy then was a lack of balance. It is believed that spring break is meant to give students a mental break from the madness—homework, exams, and other educational pressures. Not adhering to this break can ultimately lead to a breakdown. Everything in life is best with balance, which is why I suggest you have a balanced spring break your senior year.

As I walk you through more of my spring break strategies, you should apply what you feel makes the most sense to you. For example, the people you choose to connect with on LinkedIn should be based on who you need information from. One day, it can be a recruiter in your industry, and the next day, it can be an employee in your industry. My first strategy was familiarizing myself with the top recruiters in the biotechnology/pharmaceutical industry rather than connect with my university Alumni or employees of companies I wanted to work for. I reached out to recruiters because I knew most companies in my field opted to use them. Most companies in all fields do.

The Importance of Connecting with Recruiters During Spring Break

Employers search for good candidates every day of the year. As previously mentioned, their business needs do follow university schedules and thus, they couldn't care less about seniors graduating college. However, recruiters get excited about spring. They know exceptional candidates are about to flood the job market. As a senior in college, you may have heard about recruiters, and if you haven't, all the more reason why I dislike college career centers. Recruiters can also be internal employees for companies. A recruiter is an individual who works for a staffing agency on behalf of companies to identify qualified people for certain jobs. For example, let's say Nike needs an entry-level software engineer. They need someone to start quickly and may have limited time and resources for an internal talent acquisition process. They reach out to Career Savage Staffing and a few other recruiting agencies for assistance. They give their max salary amounts and tell the firms to weed out any candidates who don't meet their minimum criteria for the role. Recruiters will search every job platform for candidates. There are a lot of job searching platforms out there, but LinkedIn, CareerBuilder, Monster, Indeed, and Zip Recruiter have provided Career Savage clients the greatest success. In most cases, the same job will be posted on every job platform, so you will be okay if you opt to only use LinkedIn and Indeed.

The way you love Instagram and TikTok is the way recruiters love LinkedIn. The best and most elite recruiters, in my opinion, will use the platform. Which is why, when you send messages to people on LinkedIn over spring break, you should also message recruiters who specialize in your field of interest. If you are unsure where to find recruiters who fill positions you are interested in, Googling "[name of industry] recruiters" is an easy start. However, you may also search for recruiters on LinkedIn. There are a few other details you should know about using a recruiter.

Right-to-Represent (R2R or RTR)

Companies will often seek the services of multiple recruitment agencies for one role. If your résumé is uploaded on all the job-searching platforms, you may receive multiple emails for one role. *Beware*: If you give the first agency that reaches out the right to represent you, you are stuck with them. Even if another recruitment company comes along with a better monetary offer or benefits, they won't have the right to represent you. If you lie and tell the second or tenth company you have not yet been submitted for the role, it makes no difference.

When the recruitment agency goes to submit you, chances are, after the company reviews your application, they will go back to your recruiter and inform them "this candidate," meaning you, "has already been submitted for the role."

To avoid being stuck with your first option, wait twenty-four to forty-eight hours before giving any recruitment company the right to represent you. Some people fear that waiting twenty-four to forty-eight hours before letting a company submit them for a role will decrease their chances of getting hired. The chances of the company finding a candidate they genuinely like within two business days is slim. It's better to be submitted by a recruiter and recruiting company you like than go with an unfavorable offer.

Role Definitions

When you start applying for jobs, you naively believe that all jobs are full-time with benefits. Unfortunately, not all job offers are full-time, nor do all employers offer benefits like vacation, sick time, and high-quality insurance. The Affordable Care Act requires employers to provide you with health insurance, but that does not mean quality insurance. Of the offered roles, the three most common are contract, part-time, and full-time. When a recruiter reaches out to you, be sure to ask what type of employment it is. When you are a contracted employee, be that contract-to-hire or regular contract, you don't receive the same benefits as a full-time employee. For example, let's say a recruiter reaches out to you for a three-year contract-to-hire position with a gas company. At the end of the three years, the company can decide to either hire you as a full-time employee with benefits, extend the contract, or let you go. When you initially take the job, you will not be an employee of the gas company. You will essentially be an employee of the recruitment company, and they will lend you to their client to complete the work. If the gas company has a companywide shutdown, you don't get paid. You don't get access to the gas company's 401(k), nor do you get any of the perks they may offer their full-time and part-time employees. In this case, the recruitment agency may offer you vacation days, a 401(k), and other perks. Even if offered, it still may not be as good as what the gas company employees receive. Ninety percent of the time, it's not.

While this is a rare case, a company can also decide, at a moment's notice, that a contracted role is arbitrary, and they no longer need you. Your recruitment firm would then decide to source you to another client or let you go. For this reason and many others, contracted roles are better for college graduates than for people with families. These roles allow college seniors to jump into the job market. Most seasoned employees tend to pass up on contract jobs for more stable options.

Moreover, as a senior, you may not care about the company 401(k) plan and daycare. Finding a job, in general, takes precedence. I worked two contracted roles before becoming a full-time employee. Each position allowed me to gain employment with companies that don't generally hire new graduates. I didn't think too much about not getting paid during companywide shutdowns because working fifty weeks out of the year was better than not working at all. My 401(k) plan was decent while my health insurance was mediocre, but as a single adult, these were things I was okay with sacrificing. I knew everything was only for the moment, and as I moved up in my career, better opportunities would follow.

Many contracted positions are readily available for new graduates. While it's no one's first pick, it is a great option. As previously mentioned, the moderate instability of a contracted role is more likely to affect a person with a family than a new college graduate who is only responsible for themselves. If the contracted role is three to six months, you can take the opportunity to explore the position and move on if an extension is not possible. This is the one instance where future employers won't question why you left a role after such a short stint.

The most important thing to pay attention to in terms of contracted roles is salary. Always ask for the most they can offer. A good recruiter will push for you to receive as much as possible because they often take a percentage of your rate. However, some recruiters will attempt to keep you in the mid to low range of the salary maximum to ensure the client goes with you. If there are two equally qualified candidates, but one is asking for $60,000 per year, and the other is asking for $75,000 per year, who do you think the company will go with? They will opt for the less expensive candidate. Don't think it is better to go lower to ensure you get the job. This is the kind of mindset that gets you working the same job for thirty years. If a company wants you, they will pay the price, and if they aren't willing to pay what you believe you are worth, they aren't the right employer. Now, you may be thinking you're worth $100,000 or more straight out of college with no experience. Unless you are a software engineer, I must alert you to be realistic. While you can ask for this amount of money, if you keep getting contacted for jobs but aren't interviewing, this exorbitant beginner rate might be the reason why.

Before giving a number, ask the recruiter, "What is the maximum rate for this position?" Let's assume they say $80,000 per year.

You can then say, "Please present my résumé to the client with an $80,000 per year rate."

If they come back and say, "The client can only do $72,500," the client is interested but does not believe your experience is worth $80,000 per annum. You can now stand firm in the $80,000 and provide support for your request, or you can meet in the middle by countering with $75,000. Salary negotiations don't have to be tricky; remember to ask for more than you want and meet in the middle. You may go through this process a couple of times before receiving an offer letter with a start date. Don't lose faith. The right opportunity will find you.

When a recruiter comes to you with a part-time (PTE) or full-time employee (FTE) role, get excited. Companies are more likely to use their internal hiring process for these positions. The process is a little different compared to contracting roles. The day you sign your offer letter is essentially the day your relationship with the recruiter concludes. For example, the gas company is looking for a PTE/FTE. A recruiter would reach out to you and ask to submit you to their client. If the client likes what they could capture from your résumé, you will be interviewed. The client would then inform the recruiter they want to move forward, and the recruiter would relay the message to you. You would negotiate your salary in the same way you do for a contracted role, decide to take the job, and sign all necessary documentation. The recruiter is no longer a factor as you are now an employee of the gas company receiving all the same benefits as other employees. This type of role is ideal.

Well, That's Unfortunate

That was my spring break. Researching the role recruiters play in the job market and understanding the aspect of offers before they arrive. I felt burned out by the end of spring break, and that's why I don't advise you to do exactly what I did. I spent all spring break researching so now you don't have to.

On the long-awaited Sunday before classes resumed, I camped out in the library to prep for my upcoming wine appreciation exam. Yes, wine appreciation is a real class, and it requires real preparation. I forgot to realize that going to the library after a break is like going to a concert and trying to walk to the front. People occupied every inch of the area. All over, students were completing last-minute assignments, starting ten-page essays that were due the next day, and sharing stories about their spring break excursions. Even I can admit it's not the greatest feeling in the world to hear about all the fun things your friends did on break while you stayed home to work and study.

After re-reading about the Bordeaux vineyards in France being destroyed by Phylloxera infestations, I looked at a few wine-pairing menus and went home to prepare for the week ahead. With my spring break being everything but balanced, I often reflect on where some of my peers are now compared to where I ended up as a result of staying on course. I never let momentary fun distract me from the bigger picture (finding a job at the time). People from my graduating class are still struggling to find a job that suits them, and this is four years post-graduation. Everyone's journey is different, and I believe my beginning was then, whereas their beginning could be now or five years from now. This goes without saying: working hard while others take breaks doesn't go in vain, but you should still try to give yourself the breather you deserve. A week off likely won't dictate your success, so long as you come back focused.

The Benefits of Career Fairs

My university was notorious for spring career fairs, and until the Monday after spring break, I never knew they existed. That's because life as a freshman, sophomore, and junior doesn't require you to care about career fairs. I am sure your college/university had career fairs you never knew about, and it's likely because you never had to pay attention until now. Most seniors that day were frantically running around campus. Some skipped lectures to get interview-ready, and others came to school in their most sophisticated outfit and decided to work on their résumé at the career center. I did neither. As soon as I caught wind of the fair, I walked home in between classes to change. I wore mustard capri pants, a black blouse, and a black blazer. There was no time for extras, so I slipped on my black flats, wore my natural curls, and dashed out the door with my laptop in hand.

When attending a career fair, it's customary to bring a few copies of your updated résumé. Since I updated my résumé frequently, all I needed to do was print copies at the library and head to the fair.

As you learned in previous chapters, your résumé needs to have certain information. An employer needs little time to see a candidate's qualifications. As I did then, I will teach you how to spruce up your résumé prior to attending a career fair. Here are some basics to consider:

1. *Color choice can be a deciding factor.* If you have every color of the rainbow, you're off to a rough start. You don't want to distract employers. You want to *attract them.* Depending on your industry, it's best to stick with a max of three colors. Some social media managers and other creatives use colors like black, turquoise, and yellow. They make the right or left pane of their résumé turquoise and add yellow text on top. This allows for the wording to pop out. Then the other side of the résumé (left or right) remains white with black text. Of course, black, turquoise, and yellow are examples, and you can choose whichever three colors you think work best. The point is to limit excessive color use because no one wants to see a Skittles résumé rendition.

2. *Length can make or break you.* A résumé is not a curriculum vitae. Your résumé, especially this early in your career, should be no more than one page, front and back.

3. *An objective is important.* Anyone who ever told you an objective is not necessary lied to you. Your objective statement is what pulls the reader in. If they see what they need in those few sentences, it will entice them to read on. The more they read, the more likely you are to be called for an interview.

4. *At this stage, high school achievements are irrelevant.* As a soon-to-be college graduate, no one cares what you did in high school. Your résumé at this stage should solely reflect your college years.

5. *Catch them with keywords.* Looking up the requirements for a general role you are interested in will allow you to plug in keywords an employer may be looking for. For example, an entry-level HR posting mentions HIPPA, organization, consistency, and compliance. These are words you want to incorporate into your résumé.

6. *Aesthetics matter.* Use a legible font paired with an acceptable font size. Additionally, some creatives add a picture of themselves and even incorporate hashtags when listing their skills. Photos and hashtags are generally a turnoff for employers in certain industries; however, it is often seen as innovative in the creative space. Be mindful of what you are applying for and what styles are appropriate.

7. *Speak to your current achievements.* Draw attention to things you achieved at your place of work and at school. Employers want to know what you have done for your previous employers. If you helped implement a new document managing system at your internship, it is important you highlight that.

8. *Use academic knowledge to your advantage.* If you have limited experience, highlight coursework and anything you learned and feel comfortable applying in the workplace.

The example résumé can be used as a template to help you draft your own.

No résumé will be the same. My career fair résumé didn't have any competencies listed because I had enough work experience to explain my capabilities. I didn't have awards and achievements, but I did have certifications listed, considering I was a licensed pharmacy technician. If you speak two languages, make sure you draw attention to this capability. For this sample résumé, a skills section wasn't necessary, but for yours, it might be. Under my skills section, I didn't put basic computer skills like Microsoft Word, PowerPoint, and Excel. Rather, I put HIPPA, pharmaceutical compliance, and other skills relevant to clinical and pharmaceutical practice. The further along you are in your Career Savage journey, the more you will begin to see the difference in what is required in your résumé. Your résumé will evolve as your experience evolves.

Sally Savage

Los Angeles, CA 90210 • (310) 555-5555 • SallySavage@gmail.com

Professional Profile

Upcoming university graduate with a strong academic background in Information Technology, experienced in managing IT related projects. Self-directed and detail-oriented professional dedicated to continuous learning with an eagerness to apply learned academic principles and practices in the field. Seeking a challenging IT position with a dynamic company.

Technical Competencies:

Windows	Mac OS	MS Office
MS Office	MURAL	G Suite
JavaScript	HTML	CSS
SQL	Trello	InVision

Education

Career Savage College   **Completion May 2021**
Bachelor of Science in Information Technology & Systems
Minor: Computer Science

Professional Experience

IT Intern   **Aug 2020 – Feb 2021**
Career Savage LLC

- Performed QA testing on project(s)
- Created and designed UI mockups for senior leadership
- Provided weekly status reports and cultivated project schedule(s)
- Liaised between the project team and leadership team
- Revamped entire document management system in under 2 months
- Oversaw the status of projects and ensured deliverables were on track with initial timelines

Awards & Achievements

Suma Cum Laude   **Fall '19 & Spring '20**
Career Savage College

Using these résumé basics, I polished my résumé, printed twenty copies, and headed over to the recreational center to meet my future employer. As soon as I walked inside, I was discouraged. It felt as if the fair was curated for business and criminal justice majors. While there were healthcare corporations in the building, they sought nonscience majors only.

"What is the point of having a career fair for *all* seniors, if *all* seniors can't find a potential employer?" I asked myself.

I did a lap around the company tables, analyzing the representation for each organization. I planned on engaging with the most approachable representatives to see if I could convince them to take my résumé and pass it along to a department seeking new science graduates. Only two organizations had approachable representatives related to my degree: a neighboring prestigious university and a retail pharmacy. Considering I worked for a retail pharmacy as a pharmacy technician, I could have leveraged my experience to gain full-time employment. I approached the booth with confidence and began to engage with the rep.

After friendly introductions, I asked, "Would your organization consider hiring students with science a degree?"

"To my knowledge, we don't have any roles open for sciences majors," he said with confidence.

I spoke about my pharmaceutical experience, yet he stood firm with his position. They were only interested in business majors as regional managers. I took the hint, thanked the man for his time, and moved on. As I approached the table for the neighboring university, I thought the interaction would be like the one I just had. On the contrary, it was quite pleasant. We introduced ourselves, shook hands, and the conversation flowed naturally. He was a friendly middle-aged man who took an interest in my work experience and eloquent speech. We discussed my decision to pursue biology and the healthcare issues

I felt needed to be addressed to ensure a healthier population. I continued to discuss my pharmaceutical experience in greater detail, as well as my biggest takeaways after serving as a technician for roughly three years in clinical and retail settings. Twenty minutes flew by as a line began to form behind me. Many students were eager to engage in conversation with the rep, yet he took his time engaging with me.

He looked at me and said, "I like you. I'm not sure what it is, but there's something about you. I'm not a science guy, so I won't pretend like I know everything you just talked about, but I know people who work at the health center, and every year around this time, they hire three people interested in healthcare or public health."

I didn't exactly know what public health was at the time, and I didn't care. What I did care about was finding a job. I expressed my great interest in the position and offered him my résumé.

"Keep it and give it to other employers who need convincing," he said. "I'm already convinced."

I recited my email and phone number, shook his hand, and left the fair feeling hopeful and accomplished.

The next day, my phone rang during my 10:00 a.m. lecture. I looked at the caller ID and saw the name of the university from the career fair. I leaped from my seat and quickly ran to the door to answer the phone. A woman called from the health center asking if I had a moment to talk about a job opportunity.

I whispered to myself in the milliseconds before answering her and said, "This guy was actually serious."

"Yes, of course I can speak," I said, trying to contain my excitement.

"Okay, great. I am calling to ask if you are interested in the position."

We discussed the role, pay rate, and start date. I couldn't believe that one business day after graduating, I would be working in my field. To think it didn't come from the hundreds of job applications I submitted, but from a random guy at a career fair who wasn't even in my field. My interview was nothing more than a first impression, and I guess he was truly impressed.

After accepting the job offer birthed from the spring career fair, I made an announcement on LinkedIn and updated my profile. Immediately after announcing my new venture, recruiters began filling my messages with opportunities they had available in public health, health care, pharmaceuticals, and clinical research. While recruiters generally reached out before, the inquiries nearly doubled. As a new graduate, half the battle is having enough experience to make an employer want to hire you. Once you are hired, finding jobs thereafter becomes less complicated and stressful. *Employers desire to hire the desirable.* When it came time for me to move onto my next role, it took less than two weeks from when I interviewed to receive an offer. Searching for a job now may become tiresome and feel like a nuisance. Remember that once you secure an opportunity, the stress of searching for a job will lessen.

CHAPTER 7

Savage Solitude

"No matter what accomplishments you
make, somebody helped you."

—ALTHEA GIBSON

The woman held up a big white index card and asked, "Can you
tell me what you see?"

"I don't really see anything; it just looks like a black blob," I said.

"Okay, what about this one?"

I tilted my head to the right and said, "It kind of looks
like a frog."

She shuffled the cards and placed them on her desk. I wasn't
sure why I was being asked to describe what I saw in inkblots.
I sat in my chair quietly as she jotted notes into her fancy
black notebook.

"Ruqayyah, now I am going to give you this test, and you are
going to have thirty minutes to do the best you can. Okay?"

I replied softly, "Okay."

At the end of the thirty minutes, I walked up to her desk and handed in the exam. As the woman marked up the test and jotted down more notes in her black notebook, I knew the outcome would be less than great because I didn't complete all the questions. The allotted amount of time wasn't long enough for me to read through all the questions. She asked me a few more evaluation questions and sent me back to class. My classmates inquired about where I went. I lied to save myself from the embarrassment. I wasn't sure how to say I went to the special education building for an assessment. A few days passed before I was called up to my third-grade teacher's desk. She told me to return to her classroom with my mom after school the following day. When my mom picked me up from school, I informed her of what my teacher requested. She acknowledged the request with a level of eagerness. I knew she wanted to know the outcome of the assessment.

By the time I got to the first grade, my mom had noticed the differences between my brilliant younger sister and me. We were sixteen months apart, and my sister's cognitive advances always resulted in my parents questioning my development. By the time I reached second grade, teachers would tell my parents that, while I was delightful to have in their classroom, I was behind compared to other children. "Her reading compression is rather poor," teachers told my mom during parent-teacher conferences. At the start of third grade, my mother chose to be proactive by authorizing my elementary school to test my level of intelligence against the national average for children my age.

The next morning, when my mom dropped me off at school, I hoped for the day to go by slowly. I hated the idea of sitting in a classroom with my teachers, a psychologist, and my mother only to discuss my intellectual deficiencies. When the last school bell rang, I walked over to my backpack hook to give off the impression that I was headed home with the rest of my peers. I walked from the classroom to the front of my school and back to my teacher's classroom. I didn't want anyone knowing why I was staying after class or asking questions that would result in me answering with a lie. I sat down at a desk near my two teachers and the psychologist as we waited for my mom to enter the room.

"Hello, sorry for being late," my mom said as she ran in the door and took a seat.

My teacher stood up. "It's no worry at all." Within five minutes, they dove into detail about the results of my assessment. My teacher said, "Your daughter tested below average in every category."

My mother looked at me sitting beside her and said, "Well, what can we do to address this?"

That meeting resulted in my being enrolled in a special education program at each school I attended. My educational assessment followed me throughout elementary, junior high, and high school. I received extra time to take exams so teachers could help me read through passages. I was required to meet with a speech therapist and an educational counselor twice a week. Each time I was called out of class, my peers speculated where I was off to. Others who sat directly next to me knew where I would go because my teacher would say, "It's time to go see your special education specialist."

My parents arranged for me to have a private tutor to assist me with my homework. I was enrolled in after-school programs centered on academic success. It was honestly like being in school all the time. My mom went to great lengths to ensure I wouldn't remain behind my peers academically. She purchased every volume and variation of *Hooked on Phonics*. While I know I was extremely privileged to grow up in an environment concentrated on academic excellence, I hated being labeled a student with a learning disability. People automatically assumed I would amount to little. My parents feared I wouldn't go to college, and family friends assumed I would pursue modeling or acting. For the record, acting requires a great memory, and modeling has its own set of difficulties. It was challenging having everyone doubt my capabilities, and it only resulted in me doubting myself. For a while, I stopped trying. I relied so heavily on my accommodations that I became dependent on the extra time and assistance. By the time I reached high school, I realized I needed to use less of my accommodations to ensure I'd survive college without them. I wanted more for myself than what people expected of me.

Reflection Is Key

As you conclude your final weeks and days as a senior, it is important to reflect on your journey thus far. Recall the progress you have made with your job hunt and graduation preparation, but more importantly, the progress you've made throughout your life and the past four years. How does it feel to be almost across the finish line? Did that D on your first exam as a freshman truly destroy your life? Did you think you would be where you are today? There are many questions you should ask yourself. Reflecting on your answers will make navigating future endeavors with discernment that much easier. I can assure you, no one (including myself) envisioned I would be where I am today. It's what allows me to be ambitious and positive about achieving grand visions. I always reflect on that moment in third grade when I was diagnosed with my learning disability.

My school district's label felt like a plague to my success but ultimately, it wasn't.

During my second semester of senior year, I reflected on my initial plans as a freshman. I declared my minor in business administration. I worked closely with a CEO and CFO in high school and assumed I would enjoy pursuing the academic side of business. I was wrong. After one semester of business classes, I was completely turned off by the idea. More importantly, I felt it wasn't necessary to have the business minor, should I ever truly want to start a business or pursue business development. Retrospection is an integral part of career success. Throughout this book, I have talked about the importance of gaining experiences to guide your career decisions. Taking microeconomics was such an unpleasant experience it made me decide to remove my business minor declaration. Starting sophomore year, I began taking courses to fulfill the requirements for a psychology minor. You can reflect on past perspectives, actions, inactions, and interactions, and move forward with insight. Similar to the insight my one semester as a business minor provided me with. When I think back to some of my experiences in college and before college, I realize I learned a lot about myself, and based on those learnings, I've had better experiences navigating my career. At the end of each school year, I would reflect and move into the new year with refined motivation. I want you to take a moment to reflect on what you have experienced this year and what you learned from those experiences:

Questions for Reflection	
What did I learn this year?	
What do I wish I had done differently this year?	
What is one thing I am proud I accomplished this year?	
What do I hope to do next year that I couldn't do this year?	
What did I learn about myself and my career this year?	
Based on this year's experiences, do I need to realign my career objectives? If so, what are my new objectives?	

If you find yourself reflecting and feel you aren't where you should be, take a step back and think about how you're perceiving your position in life. A lot of our negative emotions and associations stem from how we perceive situations.

Considering you should only be competing with yourself, ponder why you feel you aren't where you should be. When you strip away the opinions of others and the status of your peers' career standing, you may notice your negative feelings dissipate. Someone will always be doing better than you and you will always be doing better than someone else. If you are still feeling negative, you're too hard on yourself. Making it through college may seem like a minor accomplishment, but rest assured, it's not. If you can't take pride in how far you have come, be proud in the fact that weeks from now, you'll be a college graduate with a higher chance of reaching the level of success you desire.

You Can Only Get Richer

Reflection should continue to be a part of your life after college. I made a lot of mistakes during my undergraduate years and even thereafter. Some mistakes I had to make repeatedly before reflecting on the insanity and ultimately changing my course of action for the better. Some of you may think reflection is harboring on past experiences. Don't confuse reflection with dwelling. You cannot change the past; you can only learn from it.

Gratitude is at the core of reflection. As it relates to my academic and career journey, not every experience has been a positive one. However, I can reflect on how unpleasant experiences have resulted in my current success. Here's one success: graduating college despite many thinking I would struggle throughout the academic system. According to the United States Bureau of Labor Statistics (BLS), only 33 percent of adults over twenty-five hold a college degree. Include in your reflection the realization that your college degree is a privilege that places you in a category of higher earning potential. We all have that friend or family member who likes to profusely state how much of a scam college is.

"It's nothing more than a way for institutions to make money," they'll say, or "You don't need college to be successful."

Colleges do make a questionable amount of money from tuition, and you don't *need* college to be successful, but the chances of you becoming successful more quickly is higher and easier with a college degree. As I mentioned in Chapter 1, in 2019, people with a bachelor's degree had an average household income of $100,164.[16] Of course, this value can increase over time with raises and promotions. Plenty of people with a bachelor's degree make six figures. Your income will also vary based on where you live and the experiences you've had as a professional. Additionally, the BLS states people with a college degree are less likely to experience unemployment. Before the global pandemic in 2019, unemployment among people with a high school diploma and no college was 5.8 percent compared to 3.1 percent among college graduates. After the pandemic, those percentages drastically increased. So, while some people in your life may antagonize you and make you feel like your degree wasn't necessary, ignore them and continue to practice gratitude. You will likely be making $30,000 more, per year, than 67 percent of adults over the age of twenty-five.[16, 17] Sure, you have student loans but when you finish paying them off, you are still left with more income than half of the adult population. It's also important to note that as more people acquire their bachelor's degree, more employers will require it. Apart from entrepreneurs, not having a college degree places you in more of an unstable position financially. Immediately after completing school, it may not feel as though your degree was worth the money, stress, and time. You may ponder the fact that you don't have a job while you are treading in debt. These moments are not permanent, and with your earnings potential increasing each year, this feeling will surely subside. Regardless of what people have to say, receiving your college degree is a great achievement that will, more likely than not, better your life.

Expressing Gratitude

What is gratitude, exactly? Gratitude requires us to look outside of ourselves and be thankful to external forces for bringing goodness into our lives—goodness that we can't achieve by ourselves. Take going to college, for example. I am grateful for my family and friends supporting me throughout my college experience because, without their love and support, I may not have completed my undergraduate education. Many people don't know I tried to drop out of college before my sophomore year. My father passed, and I lost all motivation to continue. My siblings encouraged me to stay the course, my friends supported me through my grief, and my mom did everything but enable my idea of becoming a college dropout. To this day, I thank my family and friends for this one supportive moment of many.

As another example, I continue to thank the one person who helped me get my first corporate job in high school. Without that experience, I may have never received succeeding career opportunities. There are many ways to practice gratitude. The easiest way, which happens to be my favorite, is to thank the people around you. Take a moment to think about who and what you are grateful for. Reflect on past moments, both good and bad. This single moment of reflection and gratitude isn't enough for you to reap the extended benefits. For future practice, refer to this chapter and the tips listed below.

Ways to Express Gratitude

Express Your Gratitude to Others

When people think about expressing gratitude, they think a gift is required. Sometimes a handwritten note detailing why you are grateful for the person is more than enough. Such a note can have a powerful and positive impact on a person's day. Beyond writing a note, you can randomly call, text, or FaceTime to check up on people who are important to you. These acts display your appreciation and value of the relationship. They also improve the status of your relationships.

Keep a Gratitude Journal

Spend five to ten minutes thinking about what you are grateful for. At the end of that time, write down each thought. Writing what you are grateful for reinforces positive emotions. Studies have shown that eight weeks of consistent gratitude journaling changes brain patterns that lead to greater empathy and happiness. You also can recall what you have written when you are going through difficult times. The first thing I ever wrote in my gratitude journal was, "I am grateful for my mindset." I generally think positively and know such a way of thinking is a blessing. When I experience more pessimistic thoughts, this thought of gratitude helps pulls me back into a positive mindset.

Reflect on Unfavorable Moments

You may think it's odd to meditate on bad moments, but it is a great gratitude practice. When you think about a bad experience or moment in your life and compare it to where you are in the present, you can realize how far you have come. I have experienced many unfavorable moments in my life and my career, but you will notice I use them as teachable moments for others and as a moment for me to realize how far I am from where I was.

Be Authentic

You may not always be in a gracious mood. Gratitude doesn't mean you aren't allowed to feel other emotions. If you aren't feeling grateful due to being sad, for example, you shouldn't fake it. Your lack of authenticity will only make you feel negatively about expressing gratitude. There may be days you feel exceedingly blessed, and other days you don't. Acknowledge those feelings and work your way back to feeling grateful in your own time.

PART III

FACING
REALITY

CHAPTER 8

One Degree Hotter

"Your life is your story and the adventure ahead of you is
the journey to fulfill your own purpose and potential."

—KERRY WASHINGTON

Congratulations, you graduated college! This is one of the biggest
milestones you will reach in your life, and you should be proud
of yourself for finishing. Career Savage is certainly proud of you.
You worked hard and persevered, and Career Savage hopes that
you have landed or will land the right job. You used all the right
Career Savage strategies, networked, and kept your eye on the
ball, which will yield the results you hoped or are hoping for.
It is important that you reflect on this and express gratitude for
having attended college (refer to Chapter 7). Approximately 70
percent of Americans do not have a college degree, and of that
percentage, I am certain many were not given the opportunity
to even apply. You are among the elite and educated 30 percent
of the US adult population privileged enough to possess a
bachelor's degree.

Graduating from college is a surreal feeling. You feel a wave of excitement and relief because, *hey*, you are finally done. All those late nights, tears, frustration, twenty-page papers that you felt were a waste of your time were well worth it because, in the end, you got a degree that sets you far ahead of many. I want to be real with you because that is what Career Savage is all about: honesty. You will come off your graduation high eventually, and when you do, you will feel things you've never felt before. It goes beyond feeling uncertain. If you landed a job after college, your post-graduation experience will differ slightly from someone who has not yet landed an opportunity.

Graduating With a Job

Shifting from life on campus to a studio apartment in the middle of a city certainly reminds you that you're not in college anymore. You will experience a culture shock, which is inevitable. College culture and adult life culture are two different realms. You'll go from waking up at noon every day after a long night of studying or partying to waking up at 6:00 a.m. to get ready for work in the morning. If you didn't experience life off-campus, you now have bills you are responsible for, like rent, electricity, internet, streaming services, car payment, insurance, credit cards, and, of course, your student loans after the six-month grace period. You get home at 5:00 p.m. every day, and instead of hanging out with your friends, you would rather stay in and binge-watch Netflix. Depending on where you accepted your offer, you may or may not have friends in proximity. This brings me to my next point: the unwavering feeling of loneliness you may feel with or without friends.

If you accepted a job offer in the same city you went to college in or where you grew up, you certainly will have some friends to surround yourself with. The caveat is these friends may no longer be people you can relate to. College changes you, and having an adult job will change you too. It is hard to go from talking to your coworkers about buying stocks and exploring the world to hanging out with your old friends who would rather sit around in a room and indulge in recreational activities.

If you accept a job in a new city, you may feel much lonelier. You will have to force yourself to make friends, and if you choose to do otherwise, your post-college depression will set in heavy. After graduating, I suggest you find a therapist. Don't suck your teeth or turn up your nose after reading that last sentence. I am serious. A therapist will help you through the college to real-life transition. I recommend going on psychologytoday.com and searching for a professional that best meets your needs. If you are against therapy, I suggest getting a gym membership or starting an after-work sport to keep you socially engaged. This way you will consistently be surrounded by new people and, hopefully, make new friends of like mind.

Pay close attention to this next piece of advice: You landed a job after graduation, and after a few months or a year, you grow weary of the work. You lack the excitement you once felt and feel the work is as challenging as tying your shoes. If this ever becomes the case, start implementing the Career Savage strategies you learned at the start of this book and look for a new job or new career path. Never stay at a job you hate. Don't listen to the people who tell you it looks poorly to have left a job only after a few months. Realistically, companies know that college graduates are a risk because they are in an exploratory stage of their careers. They understand this working generation and generations to come may bounce around after a few times until they find something suitable. You don't need to work the same old routine job if that is not what you want. You can do whatever you want in life. To give you more insight on when it's time to walk away from a job, here are some warning signals:

You Dread Waking Up in the Morning

The only day you wake up feeling happy is Friday because you know the workweek is over. You shouldn't be dreading the start of five out of seven days in a week. Life is far too short to be doing anything you dread or distaste. Regift yourself a purposeful and fulfilling life. Plan your escape route and leave your job as soon as possible. When I say plan your escape route, I mean you should set a deadline to leave your job or start actively looking for work in the interim. When the deadline comes, offer or no offer, you leave (but only do this if you have a savings account). Otherwise, you may find yourself at that job for another six miserable months. If you do not have a savings account, you will need to set another deadline and keep working your current job until another opportunity comes. Career Savage recommends taking risks after college but putting yourself in a financial strain isn't the kind of risk I would suggest.

You Can No Longer Tolerate Your Colleagues or Boss

While there are some expectations, there is one unspoken rule in the workforce: you should try not to publicly berate your previous employers. For that reason, I can't share which one of my previous employers asked me when I planned to remove my wig during a team meeting. If you used to ignore your boss's snarky commentary and your coworker's not-so-funny jokes, but now every time they open their mouth, you want to scream, it is time to plan your escape. Nothing has changed about them; you hate your job. If the work used to be enjoyable and distracted you from the fact that your boss is unpleasant and your coworker is borderline ignorant but now the work seems bland, it is time to plan your escape. You need to move on to a better work environment and opportunity.

You Are Late Every Day

If you hit the snooze button at 6:00 a.m., 6:30 a.m., 7:00 a.m., 7:30 a.m., 8:00 a.m., and 8:30 a.m., you need to reevaluate what keeps you in bed. You then drag yourself out of bed at 8:35, tell yourself you'll shower when you get home, hop in your car, and stroll into the office at 9:20. Your morning meeting already started, and you couldn't care less. These are signals that you may no longer love your job, and it is time for a change. This is not the life you want, and you and I both know it. Put yourself out of your misery and plan to quit.

You'll Miss Work for Anything

You would be surprised by some of the excuses I have heard people use to get out of going to work. If you are making up outlandish or ordinary excuses to miss a day of work, you surely need to evaluate your time there. If you are telling yourself you can't miss your dog's second birthday, something is off. You tell yourself your car is on empty and stopping at the gas station will make you five minutes later than usual, so what's the point of going into the office? If you convince yourself that you are seriously ill because you woke up innocently sneezing, something is off with these scenarios, and it's time to reevaluate your employment.

You Start Making Careless Mistakes

You have stopped reading your emails before sending them out to people. Who cares if you spelled the client's name wrong, right? *Wrong.* If you keep making careless errors, you will likely tarnish your name within your profession. Remember, when you apply for another job, they ask for references. Do you want your next employer to think you are a careless person? No. It's best you walk away from this job while your reputation is still intact.

These are not all the signs, and ultimately you will know when to leave a job. You know yourself better than anyone else, so if you are miserable and you know your job is the cause of that, plan your escape. While planning your escape, assess your finances and ensure you have another opportunity on the horizon.

Graduating Without a Job

If you have not yet landed a job, take a moment to breathe. Don't go having panic attacks every day and living with a cloud of negativity over your head. Stay the course and continue to follow the Career Savage strategies you have been following. You will surely find a job. You will, however, need to step up your networking game. You will also need to actively pay attention to your email. Every morning when you pick up your phone, turn off that irritating buzzing (your alarm) and to check your email, *not TikTok or Instagram.* Not Twitter, Snapchat, Facebook, or any other social media account that has nothing to do with benefiting your career. Get excited to wake up in the morning and see what job offers, professional development opportunities, and personal development opportunities await in your inbox. Ignore or delete everything from Shop Runner to those silly weekly email subscriptions you have and start reading through the job offers presented. Even if the job does not match your criteria, connect with the recruiter and let them know the job is not a good fit but keep you in mind for other opportunities. If you still are having trouble, which I humbly doubt you will, contact Career Savage. If you do have a job that is simply not one you hope to keep, please consider all your financial obligations before quitting the job you had during your college years.

Graduating college without having a full-time job means you will feel uncertain, but it doesn't mean you should risk it all unless you are financially stable enough to do so. A few Career Savage clients graduated and did not receive a job offer until two to three months later. So again, stay the course. In addition, you may feel sad to see others getting job offers or simply sad you are not where you planned to be. One, don't compare yourself to other people, and two, you are exactly where you are supposed to be. The right job will come at the right time. Lastly, you may experience the same loneliness those who graduated with a job feel. Post-college depression is a real thing. You have to adjust to a new lifestyle. You will experience the same reevaluation of friendships and reevaluations of self that graduates with offers feel. Again, I recommend looking for a therapist that best meets your needs to help you through your transition.

Outside of having a therapist to help you cope with the stress of post-graduation, you will need to go above and beyond in fine-tuning your job searching and interviewing skills. The most common text I receive from college graduates with no job offer is, "I keep getting called in for interviews but receive no offers." No one teaches young people how to sell themselves in an interview, which is why this dilemma exists. That is what an interview is all about. Why should the employer hire you of all candidates? What do you bring to the table that will better the company culturally and financially? Many people could be the perfect candidate but simply get nervous when sitting across the table from strangers or over a video call. If this is you, you seriously need to practice.

Career Savage offers interview preparation sessions where you will be asked the same questions an employer may ask. If you do not get nervous, you need to practice coming off confident without over-selling yourself. Both the nervous and the confident need to prepare for interviews. Before every interview, you need to request the names of the people who will be interviewing you. After you receive their names, it is time to cyber-study them and their experiences. Search their LinkedIn profiles for any points you can connect with them on. For example, I interviewed with the president of my former employer. Naturally, before my interview, I searched for her LinkedIn profile and found that she too pursued her MPH (master's in public health). I brought up this point during my interview and simply asked if she felt having a master's in public health helped her better assimilate into her role as president of a pharmaceutical company. She seemed surprised that I even bothered to ask, and from there, we engaged in a ten-minute discussion on the benefits of a master's degree and how she felt about pursuing hers. This company interviewed ten people after me and did not like any of them. I was the first candidate they interviewed for the role. After being hired, I came to find out the president loved that I asked that question and thought I was a memorable and persistent candidate.

My point? Find information that ties back to your educational background and/or career experiences and mention them during your interview. If you are to meet with five people, you better research all of them. After you are done searching for your interviewers, you will need to research the company. Familiarize yourself with simple facts. When did the company open? What is the company's mission? Research the company to give yourself a better understanding as to why you even want to work for them. What about the company makes you excited to wake up in the morning and go to work? When you already have this information in your head, your enthusiasm will translate into the interview. You need to speak passionately about the role, industry, and company. Many people will not do this and simply go into the interview with a different attitude. If it translates into the interview that you are only there because you need a check or something to do, the employer can tell, and guess what? They won't hire you.

After researching the interviewers and the company, you now need to shop for an interview outfit. Let me stop here and stress to you the importance of a proper business outfit for in-person interviews. I have interviewed people for jobs at my previous places of employment. I try not to evaluate a candidate based on what they are wearing, but if you walk in with a wrinkled t-shirt and khaki shorts, I can't promise not to mark that against you. My colleague and I were asked to interview a candidate for a general position at our company. She went in first, I followed, and then we met to discuss the candidate's qualifications. We both felt the candidate was lackluster, showing little interest in the position and, in addition, was dressed as if attending a concert. They even wore sunglasses on their head as if they just left the beach and decided to pop into the interview. On paper, they were fine. They met the qualifications for the job, but the way they presented themself was unprofessional. I promise you this, if they had come in wearing a pair of slacks, a button-down, and removed the sunglasses, we would have both voted to onboard them. However, their nonchalant attitude matched their outside appearance, which would translate into their work style.

Some people will say it's ridiculous to judge a person based on the clothes they wear. I have to agree, it is ridiculous, but ridiculous does not always mean untrue. In the professional setting, you can judge a person based on what they wear to their interview because first impressions are everything. A person with unkempt or unprofessional interview attire will more likely than not be lazy. If you can't put five minutes into looking presentable, why should I believe your work won't complement your presentation? It is crazy to think not wearing the proper clothing cannot get you a job, but I have seen it happen. Outside of people I have interviewed, I have heard colleagues come out of an interview and comment on candidates' hygiene and clothing choices for an interview outfit. Let me say that whether it is right or wrong, employers talk about you when you leave, and they discuss everything from the fluff in your résumé to the shoes on your feet. This is why you need to be mindful of your appearance when going to an interview. For some job interviews, you can dress down. For example, if you are interviewing to become a personal shopper, you probably don't need to go in with a blazer and slacks. A pair of jeans may be deemed acceptable. Regardless, depending on your industry, you should research what to wear.

You don't have to break the bank to create an interview outfit. The point is to have a professional outfit in your closet always awaiting to be worn. Here is a list of ten stores that sell moderately affordable professional clothing items for all genders:

1. J.Crew
2. J.Crew Factory
3. Zara
4. H&M
5. Nordstrom
6. Nordstrom Rack
7. Banana Republic
8. Bloomingdale's
9. Gap
10. Macy's

You now know that you need to do before interviewing: research your interviewer, research the company, and get a professional outfit. Let's circle back to rehearsing your interview. If you opt not to contact Career Savage, you will need to know what questions to ask and what questions you must know the answers to. You should, of course, know every inch of your résumé. As mentioned earlier, submit a truthful résumé because fabrication will cause you to slip up when asked to speak in detail about a previous job or task you said you completed. Employers know when you are lying, especially if you are interviewing for a technical job. And again, know why you want to work for the company. It has never failed me to be prepared to answer that question.

Before you go into your interview, you must also have questions prepared for your interviewer. My favorite question to ask is the *savage 3-3-3*. "What do you expect me to complete or achieve in my first three days, three weeks, and three months?" I never say three years because I can't promise an employer I will be with them for that length of time. If you ask this question at the end of the interview, I guarantee the hiring manager will be pleased with your initiative to establish goals before even getting an offer. You may think three days is too short a time to complete anything, but the task could be something as simple as uncovering the root cause of a poor system/process. When you come prepared with questions, it tells the employer that you are also interested in what the company has to offer. When someone comes prepared for an interview with specific questions, I believe the candidate knows their value and wants to make sure the company is also a great fit for them, not just the other way around. If you truly have no questions, you did zero homework because I know the research you were supposed to do would generate at least *one* question. It is important to note that while you may want answers to some human resource questions, you should not be asking about that until you are extended an offer. Here are typical questions you should and should not ask during an interview:

Do Ask

- Can you elaborate on the company culture?
- Regarding the team I will be working on, can you speak to the management style?
- How would you describe the team dynamic?
- What is the biggest challenge that someone in this position would face?

- Is there anything you have seen on my résumé or realized during this interview that would cause concern for my success in this role?

Do *Not* Ask

- How long does it take to get a raise?
- When is the earliest I can take a vacation?
- What percentage do you contribute to my 401(k)?
- Am I required to work late?

Some of these questions, like the one regarding your 401(k), can be asked after an offer has been made; if human resources interviews you, you can ask them. Otherwise, you will come off as a candidate more concerned about money than contributing to the company. You can find more questions to ask at themuse. com or by googling "questions to ask during an interview." As a college graduate looking for work, you now know what to do to prevent the "interviews but no offers" phenomenon.

How to Avoid the "Interviews but No Offers" Phenomenon

1. Practice interviewing.
2. Research the company you are interviewing with.
3. Research interviewers.
4. Prepare questions to ask.
5. Purchase or put together professional outfit.

Job or no job, life after graduation goes far beyond looking for employment. It's funny how no one talks to young people, especially pre-graduates, about interviews, budgets, taxes, life goals, credit, or the importance of self-care and maintaining your mental health. Actually, it's not funny; it's frustrating. It is far more important to be educated on these items than some of the frivolous courses students must take. How has Music 101 ever helped me in my career? It hasn't, and I have never once had a conversation with people in my field about Mozart being one of the greatest composers of all time. Mozart doesn't get you a higher credit score. Mozart also can't teach you how to file your taxes. I know colleges may feel it isn't their place to educate students on topics that will better their life and future, but I beg to differ. Those who attend college generally are between the ages of eighteen and twenty-two, freshly released from high school. High school is not meant to prepare you for the workforce, but college is. In being prepared for the workforce, one would expect to learn about 401(k)s, IRAs, and the difference between an HMO and PPO insurance plan. Or at least how to negotiate salaries. This is why you are reading a *Career Savage* book, so I can tell you a few important things you need to know as a college graduate.

Remote Work Isn't for Everyone

Remote working has become the new way of living. During the COVID-19 pandemic, hundreds of companies and organizations were required to let their employees work from home. Before the pandemic, organizations feared employees would neglect their responsibilities because of in-home distractions and lack of interest in work. What companies realized was employees worked more efficiently and productively at home. Companies like Twitter even decided to make their work-from-home policy permanent, post-pandemic.

As a new graduate and working professional, working from home sounds like the best of both worlds. If you enjoy traveling, you can globetrot and support yourself at the same time. While it sounds amazing (and believe me, it is), working from home is *not* for everyone. Do not accept a 100 percent remote role if you know you are the type of person to neglect your responsibilities for a trip to the mall or an all-day movie fest. Working from home requires a high level of concentration and discipline. You are the only person who can hold yourself accountable while working remotely. You can also work more hours than in an office setting. It is also extremely challenging to separate work life from your personal life, as it often becomes merged into one. As soon as you realize your personal life and work life have become intertwined, you should incorporate boundaries. However, even with boundaries, the lines can continue to blur.

Unless you are required to do these things per your offer letter, answering work emails, texts, and phone calls after working hours or on the weekends is a prime example of *blurred lines*. Waking up at 6:00 a.m. and skipping the opportunity to groom yourself to get a head start on your day is an example of *blurred lines*. Working in your bed for twelve hours straight, skipping much-needed meals to answer "one more email" is another example of *blurred lines*. You may think these examples are extreme, but they happen easily in a work-from-home setting. As I navigated my first remote job, I found myself in these situations almost daily. As a result, I've learned remote working can be done healthily if you choose to be conscious about it. If you get the chance to work from home, you will need some tips to help you navigate your new lifestyle. Below are my top three tips for healthy remote working.

Set Boundaries

Waking up, opening your laptop, and starting your day is the first sign you're headed in the wrong direction. Whether you live in a studio apartment or your parents' house, your bedroom should be where you rest and receive peace of mind. Working from your bed mentally changes how you perceive the space. It becomes less of a place to rest and more of a space for productivity. Setting the boundary to work outside your bedroom or simply out of your bed will give your mind the perception that work and home are separate entities.

When you wake up and start your day, don't let your laptop be the first thing you open. Turn on the shower, unscrew your toothpaste cap, do anything to signify you are getting ready for the workday. Just because you aren't going to the office doesn't mean you shouldn't *get ready* for work. The act of getting ready will put you in the mental space of thinking you are leaving to do something. This is why I mention working outside your room or sleep space. If you get ready and leave one space to work in another, work and home become separate, creating a necessary boundary.

Another aspect of setting boundaries is knowing when to engage in work-related matters. The do-not-disturb feature on electronics is useful for setting timing boundaries. Depending on your role within your organization, there may be days where you are required to answer some correspondence outside of business hours. For entry-level, junior, and some mid-senior level positions, this is unlikely. You should form the habit of waiting for hours of operation to respond. Answering an email at two, three, or four in the morning encroaches on your sleep time and personal life. Everyone wants to be a good employee, but don't be duped into believing good employees don't have boundaries.

Set a Schedule for Yourself

When you work remotely, you can often set your hours of operation with respect to the organization's general hours of operation. Working for a global organization means they are likely twenty-four hours. If you work with global colleagues, your days may start as early as six in the morning. In this case, wake up at five and get ready to start your day. Starting at six in the morning certainly means your day ends at 3:00 p.m. The difficulty in starting early and ending early is feeling the need to stay on beyond your required nine hours. A local colleague may request to meet with you at four in the afternoon, and you may feel obligated to attend. Stand firm in declining meetings outside your set working hours. You can also block your calendar to ensure no one schedules meetings outside your time preferences. Sticking to a schedule, like a schedule you would have in an office setting, gives you space to have time to yourself. Working from home increases the probability of burnout, which is why time to yourself is instrumental in keeping you productive and interested in your job.

Change Your Scenery

A change in scenery gives your brain a subtle reset. If you ask remote workers where they enjoy working, they will give you a long list of coffee shops, lounges, and workspaces. It's unlikely they suggest working at home every day. For the record, working from home doesn't mean you *always* have to be in your house. You can work in every area of your home and grow tired of eating, sleeping, and working in one space. It feels as though you are trapped in a work continuum. If you are able, attempt to change your scenery once a week.

Remote working has its pros and cons like anything else in the world. Ultimately, you will choose what works best for you. Before COVID-19, remote internships and entry-level positions were unheard of. Ninety percent of what makes internships and entry-level jobs so great is the in-person exposure you receive. If you receive a remote offer and can work inside the office, do both. No amount of Zoom calls can equate to the valuable exposure you would receive in an office setting. From conference meetings to hallway conversations, you miss out on moments that are instrumental in your career growth. Working remotely is great, but it can still negatively influence your career growth in the end.

Friends Come, and Friends Go

I used to think the friends I've made throughout my life I had to keep forever. If you have never heard this saying before, let me be the first person to tell you, you don't need to keep every friend you've ever made in your life. After graduating college, I realized friends would come and friends would go. People who are meant to remain in your life for a long time will organically remain in your life. Your visions may not be the same, but your ambitions, values, beliefs, and/or thought processes will align. There will be some form of commonality among the people who remain. As a new graduate afraid of change, I held onto friendships that did not serve me but rather detracted from my life, whether mentally or in another way. I allowed myself to hold onto stressful relationships that pulled me further away from what I wanted for my life. I was friends with many unmotivated people. While there is nothing wrong with being comfortable or being okay with being *okay*, this was not who I was nor ever will be. Whether spiritual, personal, or professional, I am always searching for ways to learn and grow. Before, I assumed the people I let into my life wanted the same, and I was wrong. Your friends may not always want the same things as you, but having common ground is what sustains friendships. Among my unmotivated friends, we had no common ground.

Before college graduation, I never realized the importance of taking inventory of your life and who is in it. I wish I knew then, but I know now, which is why I need you to understand the importance of this message. You have to excuse from your life those not contributing positive energy or any energy that motivates you to be a better version of who you once were. Many people are stuck in a cycle of toxicity or complacency and won't realize it until they take inventory of themselves and their friendships. Your job, friends, extracurriculars, relationships, living situation, even family members can be toxic. Many people will act as a mere distraction from your life goals, which you'll only realize after taking inventory of your relationships. All this to say, friends come and go; if some come while not contributing anything positive to your life, you need to be the one to let those friendships go, no matter how difficult it may seem.

Write Down Life Goals

Your goals don't stop because you graduated; they merely evolve. You should have low-, medium-, and high-level goals that you optimize every three to six months or as needed. Graduating college was probably your high-level goal and now you are unsure what goals you need to set, if any at all. This sometimes scares people and shifts them into a dark place as they feel a level of chaos. For example, if you plan to go back to school, then your next high-level goal should be receiving an acceptance. Your medium-level goal would be working on and completing your application in a set time frame, and your low-level goal would be all the granular tasks required to meet your medium- and high-level goals. If you are not planning to go back to school, your goal-setting would be a lot less structured.

Assuming you desire to immediately begin working in your field after graduation, your first high-level goal should be receiving an offer and maintaining your job for at least six to twelve months. If you are miserable at that job, within the first couple of months, you should be planning to leave and reset your goals. If you already have a job you love, your high-level goal could be receiving a promotion or raise. Your medium-level goal would be assuming more responsibility at your place of employment, and your low-level goals would be all the tasks required to reach your medium- and high-level goal. The point of goal-setting is to keep you on track, ensuring you are en route to arrive where you want to be in life. It is advised that you create goals for three months, six months, one year, and three years. Setting a three-year goal allows you to work toward your bigger picture, but if three years is too far out for you, you can skip it. You should have goals for your job, goals for your side hustle, goals for your education, and goals for personal development. Don't feel you have to have only one goal you are focused on. All these goals are attainable as long as you refer to your set goals along your journey. For reference, this is how your goals can appear:

Career

Starting: *March 2022*	
Three-Month Goal(s)	• Apply to five jobs per day • Upload résumé bi-monthly on job platforms • Practice interviewing • Attend one networking event per month • Update LinkedIn and message connections
Six-Month Goal(s)	• Receive an offer for a well-paying job ($60k/annum at minimum)
One-Year Goal(s)	• Receive a raise and promotion to manager • After raise is received, continue to exceed employers' expectations by taking on more responsibilities
Three-Year Goal(s)	• Become a senior manager within my industry

Education

Starting: *March 2022*	
Three-Month Goal(s)	• Research programs of interest • Have letters of recommendation ready
Six-Month Goal(s)	• Complete school applications • Complete personal statements • Take GMAT, MCAT, or LSAT
One-Year Goal(s)	• Receive admissions to doctorate or master's program
Three-Year Goal(s)	• Graduate from school with job in place

Side Hustle

Starting: *March 2022*	
Three-Month Goal(s)	• Start Instagram and TikTok accounts for business • Build website and launch brand • At minimum, network once a week to gain clients
Six-Month Goal(s)	• Purchase LLC • Have passive income of $250 per month • Get business cards
One-Year Goal(s)	• Have passive income of $500 per month
Three-Year Goal(s)	• Have passive income of $2,000 per month

Personal Development

Starting: *March 2022*	
Three-Month Goal(s)	• Practice one new Italian word each day • Save $25 a week for trip to Rome
Six-Month Goal(s)	• Complete Italian 101
One-Year Goal(s)	• Speak Italian fluently • Begin planning solo trip to Rome
Two- to Three-Year Goal(s)	• Solo travel to Rome

Now that you have seen an example, it's time to write down some goals for yourself. Fill out the charts on the next pages with goals you want to accomplish in the following four areas of your life.

Career

Starting:	
Three-Month Goal(s)	
Six-Month Goal(s)	
One-Year Goal(s)	
Three-Year Goal(s)	

The Prepared Graduate

Education

Starting:	
Three-Month Goal(s)	
Six-Month Goal(s)	
One-Year Goal(s)	
Three- to Four-Year Goal(s)	

Side Hustle

Starting:	
Three-Month Goal(s)	
Six-Month Goal(s)	
One-Year Goal(s)	
Three-Year Goal(s)	

Personal Development

Starting:	
Three-Month Goal(s)	
Six-Month Goal(s)	
One-Year Goal(s)	
Two- to Three-Year Goal(s	

When you write down your goals, it reminds you of what you are working toward. Without setting goals in life, you are simply working aimlessly. While some people can do this, Career Savage will always advise setting goals to avoid forgetting your bigger picture.

Pick Up Those Life Skills

A former coworker told me decision-making was a true talent. I could not believe they considered making decisions was a skill. All you have to do is decide on whatever it is you want, and that's it. After working professionally for a few more years, I realized they were right. Some people cannot make up their minds and decide on one thing (or anything, for that matter). This may be something that resonates with you if you too struggle with making up your mind, and I can't blame you. You went from preschool to elementary school to junior high to high school and then college. You may have never had to make any decisions for yourself. To graduate college and now be responsible for making all decisions regarding your life can feel overwhelmingly paralyzing. This is why you now need to exercise making executive decisions in your life. When posed with deciding, don't run to your parents. Sit down, weigh the pros and cons of each option, and decide what is best for you. The first few choices you make may not be the best, but in the end, you will get better at deciding what is better for *your life*.

Another skill you should work on is communication. Some people have horrible communication skills. They are unable to handle confrontation, unable to voice their emotions, and unable to truly convey information verbally, written, or even through their body language. Don't let this be you. Poor communication skills will land you a first-class ticket to nowhere. Decision-making and communication are two of the most important skills you need to be successful. You also need to have impeccable coping skills for two reasons. Firstly, rejection and success go hand in hand. Begin training your mind to be okay with rejection. This way, you won't feel discouraged when faced with a "no" or an opposing opinion to your idea. Secondly, change accompanies success. Having excellent coping skills will allow you to embrace change rather than fear it. You will come across complacent people who cannot achieve their aspirations, and the answer for this complacency is almost always fear. You need to work on many life skills after graduating college. Such skills will eventually translate into your professional and personal relationships. You know yourself better than anyone; therefore, you should know what life skills you need to fine-tune. For those stuck on what skills to begin working on, here is a list of skills Career Savage finds important for success after graduation:

Top Five Savage Life Skills

1. Decision-making
2. Effective communication
3. Active listening
4. Coping
5. Self-awareness

Budgets Are Your Friend

You can attempt to avoid your student loans, but eventually, whomever you borrowed the money from will come to collect. By now, you should know the six-month grace period most financial institutions grant won't last forever. Knowing this, you should no longer feel free to frivolously swipe your debit card every morning at your favorite artisanal coffee shop when you can make your own. Even if you were fortunate enough to attend college and avoid student loan debt by way of your trust fund, scholarships, or loan forgiveness, you should still recognize that budgets are your friend and avoid spending money you're better off saving.

Let us assume you got the job you had been hoping for, and you are now making $70,000 per year while living in Los Angeles. After federal and state taxes, you likely take home approximately $51,886 per year or $4,323 per month. This amount does not consider extra deductions you may have because of your 401(k) or health insurance. If you have rent, utilities, transportation fees, student loans, and credit card payments, you will likely shell out approximately $3,000 per month on bills alone. This is with the assumption you are living in a studio apartment. This leaves you with approximately $1,332. In addition to those fixed costs, you will need to buy groceries, among other necessities, which may cost you anywhere from $250 to $500 per month. Now, worst-case scenario, you are left with $1,000. In 2020, $67,000 per year was the median household income.[22] And $70,000 is still above the average US median household income and a decent amount of money for a single college graduate who has not started a family. With this type of salary, depending on the city you live in, you should be more than okay financially to pay your rent, take care of your other bills, save, and live a youthful life.

Budgets may sound unappealing, but once you begin saving and chipping away at your debt, you will feel differently. When you have less debt, two things happen: (1) your credit score goes up, and (2) financial institutions will feel more comfortable loaning you more money should you need it. Why is this important? Assuming you want to own a house one day, with excellent credit, you will gain access to better mortgage rates. Beyond the mortgage rates, good credit benefits you and opens the door to more financial opportunities. Of course, budgeting is much easier said than done. Here is an outline of the percentages you should be spending on certain items:

Budget Table*	
Rent (25% or less)	**$1,458**
	If you live in an overpopulated city (i.e., Los Angeles, New York City, or San Francisco) where rent is extremely high, get a roommate. You just graduated from college—right now is not the time to "flex." Do *not* spend more than 25 percent of your income, before taxes, on rent. If you are making $70,000 per year, your rent maximum is approximately $1,460 per month.
	You may be tempted to live on your own or in a newly remodeled apartment. Do not allow your ego to eat a hole in your wallet. If you can move in with your parents, do so. If not, shop for a roommate and the most budget-friendly accommodation.
	You can visit rentcafe.com to calculate how much you should spend on rent based on your annual income.

Savings (10% or more)	~ $585 Saving approximately $585 per month equates to $7,020 a year. Did you know most Americans have less than $1,000 saved for emergencies? Apart from unforeseen circumstances, this is the result of excessive consumerism and/or a lower income. You should be saving, at the minimum, 10 percent of what you make. If you are unable to do so, save as much as you can.
Student Loans (10%)	~ $585 The financial institution that loaned you money to go to school will likely make your monthly payments 10 percent of your monthly income. They do this so the interest accrues, and they make more money in the end. You should pay as much as you can every chance you get. Financial gurus will tell you to pay off student loans before saving any money, but Career Savage disagrees. It is always good to have money saved for a rainy day. Either way, ensure 10 percent of what you make is allotted for your student loan debt.

Credit Cards	-
	Credit cards are dangerous, and for this reason, I advise you to not use credit unless you know how to manage your money. Considering you are a new college graduate, you likely have no idea the trouble credit cards can put you. A credit card is money you *do not* have. You are required to pay all the money you use at the end of the month, or they charge you a disgusting amount of interest. Now, if you are responsible (and this is a big *if*), you should use your credit card for everything you would use your debit card for and pay the balance off every month. This way, you accrue free points and money. I would also only advise using your card to pay for things that you already budgeted for.
Food (6% or less)	**$350** You should spend approximately 6 percent of your income on groceries each month. Anything more and you are likely splurging unnecessarily.

Transportation (15% or less)	$875 If you make $70,000 per year, you should spend no more than $10,500 per year or $875 per month on transportation fees. If you live in a city with great public transportation, your fees may be lower. If you live in a city that requires driving, you should be mindful that this monthly amount includes a car payment, maintenance, gas, and insurance. When you buy your car after graduating, do not go and buy a BMW, Mercedes, or Range Rover. You will be living way above your means if you do so. Such luxurious cars require expensive maintenance and consume a lot of gas. Think realistically within this budget when searching for a car.
Entertainment (5% or less)	$291 Entertainment includes everything from bar-hopping with friends to movie nights with a partner. Having a cap will allow you to set boundaries and tell people no. If you max out your entertainment fund for the month, you must wait until the following month to resume any entertaining activities. Don't dip into the following month.

This example is based on a $70,000 annual salary and does not include deductions that may occur as a result of your 401(k) and health insurance.

After budgeting out your monthly salary, you are still left with a few hundred dollars. Good financial practices call for you to leave this extra money in your checking account and build more liquid cash in addition to your savings. However, you can also choose to add the remainder to your entertainment budget or whichever category you feel is most important to you.

Building Financial Wealth

In addition to having a budget, you should take time to optimize your finances. Apply for credit cards that will benefit you and begin or continue building your credit. If you travel a lot, applying for a travel card would be to your benefit. If you eat out often, using a credit card that offers cash back for restaurants would be worth your while. The problem with credit cards is people don't know how to manage them. If you are poor with managing your money, don't apply for five credit cards you plan to abuse. Having credit cards builds your credit, which, in turn, contributes to building your wealth. When you are ready to purchase a home or do anything that requires institutional loans, your credit will be one of the most important factors for approval.

Liquid cash is as important as credit, real estate, and other investments. With your liquid assets, you should opt to put a bulk amount of money in a high-yield savings account. My preference is the Marcus Goldman Sachs savings account. General savings accounts offer 0.01 percent, whereas high-yield saving accounts offer market value. Interest rates can go beyond 1 percent, as the rate is highly dependable on the status of the economy. Even though the profit you will gain from a high-yield savings account is not nearly as much as you would gain from the stock market, having your money in a high-yield account is better than having it in a basics savings account that only yields 0.01 percent in annual profit.

As a postgraduate, learning how to manage your money can be overwhelming. You don't need to make all these changes in one day. You can take time to decide what works best for you. As an easy starting guide, it is advised you begin with closing or upgrading any account you received because you were a college student. College accounts don't offer any benefits to working professionals. If you have a college checking account, inquire with your bank or other banks offering higher interest rates about what they have to offer. My favorite is Charles Schwab. They offer a brokerage account with each checking account, allowing you to use excess money to invest in the stock market. Before you get carried away and think I am advising you to invest all your savings in the S&P 500, understand that the stock market is risky. Whatever money you put in, don't expect to see that money in less than five years. Some people view their stock market investments as money they will never see again. Keep in mind your 401(k) account, offered by your employer, invests money in the market for you. Until you are comfortable with playing with your excess savings, you can rest assured knowing some of your assets somewhere are multiplying.

Contrary to popular beliefs, I genuinely don't believe everyone needs to start their own business while working a nine-to-five to be successful or obtain wealth. Everyone in our generation is caught up with meeting society's expectations, which allows them to forget why they are doing what they do in the first place. Their career journey then becomes a chase for money rather than a working desire to fulfill one's purpose. If wealth is a success factor for you, you don't have to start a business. You can acquire quite a bit of wealth working a traditional job. From 401(k) matching to company equity, wealth can be obtained. As a new employee, I wasn't sure what a 401(k) was. I spent hours researching how to maximize my benefits and realized a 401(k)-match program is essentially free money. In 2020 and 2021, the IRS allowed employees to put $19,500 in their 401(k). So, if you opt to put $19,500 per annum of pre-tax or taxed money into your retirement account, your employer may match that and put $19,500 in as well. That's $39,000 saved in one year. The actual amount depends on what percentage of your salary you opt to put in and what percentage your company will match. The money that sits in your 401(k) is invested in the market, and over the years, you see the number grow. Should you leave an employer, you can carry over that balance to your next 401(k) account. This is one aspect of building your wealth as a traditional employee.

When I first started working, I always knew the real way to make money in corporate America was to a) negotiate, b) leverage, and c) build a case for promotion. My first salaried job offered me $50,000 per year with benefits. As a twenty-two-year-old college graduate, I thought I hit the jackpot. Even though I was elated, I wanted to make my first attempt at negotiating for more. I went back to my recruiter and asked for $59,000. He came back and said $57,000 was the highest they could offer. Considering my rent was $300, my car payment was $250, and my car insurance was $100, I couldn't believe I managed to negotiate so much extra income. The more I worked in corporate America, the more I learned. For one, promotions won't always come. You must either fight for it or plot for one and if it doesn't come from within your place of employment, you can secure an opportunity within another organization. After leaving my first place of salaried employment, I was on to bigger and better things, receiving a 41 percent salary increase. This was the biggest increase I had ever acquired. While the numbers looked good, this job came with its own set of downsides. My commute was three hours one way, and I paid for 40 percent of my health insurance. When you subtract the amount of money I spent on gas and car maintenance, the salary increase leveled out to about 13 percent. For this reason, I decided to take a large pay cut and accept a different opportunity that had virtually no commute. I worked for this employer for one year and a half while pursuing my master's in public health.

After one year and a half, I found myself drowning in responsibilities without being adequately compensated for the work I was doing. No one cared to develop me, and I strongly disliked the management style of my director. Poor management is always a great reason to leave a job. Once I received my master's degree, I left my employer and saw another major jump in my salary as I started to make headway in the six-figure range. I always set the milestone to make six figures by twenty-five, and with resilience, I was able to. This was my fifth employer since graduating college less than three and a half years ago. Many people would classify this as job-hopping. They will tell you working for too many people makes you look like an unstable employee. It makes employers hesitant when considering hiring you because they see each hire as an investment. Why invest in someone who will likely leave in six months to two years? This way of thinking is quite archaic as employers are adapting to the lifestyles of Millennials and Generation Z.

Promotions and raises won't always be mutually exclusive, especially at smaller organizations. As you work your way through corporate America, you will learn to have little expectations of your employers. It's up to *you* to advocate for yourself. The goal of your employer is to make as much money as possible while spending as little as possible. Some employers make millions to billions in revenue and may not care to penny-pinch on employee salaries, but you never know. When you receive a promotion, make sure the title change is accompanied by a salary increase of at least 20 percent. Ideally, new responsibilities should reach 30 percent, but you should use discretion to ensure your new salary is sound within your industry. If you feel the increase matches market offers, then you're okay to accept.

The job market changes with each generation. Millennials and Generation Z aren't like ones preceding. We don't stay with employers out of obligation or loyalty. We see employment as a mutually beneficial relationship. You will see that people who have obtained some wealth through a traditional job have worked for more employers than they can count. My fifth employer, let's say ABC Consulting, was a small boutique firm offering consulting services within my industry. During my two years with ABC Consulting, I received one title change and three significant raises: 12.5 percent, 15 percent, and finally 7.6 percent. As a note to self, anything under 10 percent should spark interest in looking for opportunities outside your organization. When you move to another organization, you will get anywhere from 10 to 30 percent.

ABC Consulting knew how ambitious I was and wanted to ensure the micro-raises received would suffice and prevent me from leaving. Be aware of this. If you feel you are under-compensated for the work you are doing, speak up. If your employer chooses to ignore your outcry, plan your exit. Once you receive offers from other companies and plan to prepare your two weeks' notice, your employer may try to get you back—but don't go back. A company should never wait to fight for you on the day you plan to announce your resignation. It can be difficult to leave a job you are emotionally tied to. That was always my downfall, leaving a company I felt I had too many personal ties to. What I have learned is there are few emotions in career advancement. There is passion, grit, and determination, but emotional decisions are few and far between. Making an emotional career decision can prevent you from acquiring the success and wealth you deserve.

Navigating Career Growth

The best careers are determined by your ability to invest in four things: relationships, skills, character, and hustle. Throughout this guide, the notion of networking has been thrown around quite a few times. As you navigate through your career, you will begin to fully understand why networking is crucial for advancement. Recommendation letters, job offers, school acceptances, personal growth, and a million other benefits are birthed in nurtured relationships. Becoming known in your industry takes time, but becoming so reputable that people seek you for advice or turn to you with top market opportunities only happens when you have a strong network. Otherwise, industry experts wouldn't know the difference between you and the next subject matter expert.

Your skills and character are things you work to refine as you evolve professionally, but hustle is what makes you a *Career Savage*. You are capable of advocating for yourself and believing in your skill set. You understand what you bring to the table, so you can hustle your way up the corporate ladder possibly quicker than people would anticipate. Despite what other people believe, you follow your course of action and understand the career growth you see for yourself may not align with others' vision for you.

While you are beginning to learn about the professional world, there will come a time when speaking the language of a Career Savage is like second nature. One aspect of being a Career Savage is understanding the amount of money a job offers doesn't necessarily correlate with career growth. Sometimes a higher dollar amount is thrown in the face of newer graduates and they don't understand the true meaning behind the higher price tag. As starting points for navigating your growth, these are things you should always think about when considering job offers.

What's Your Commute?

I used to commute three hours daily, one way, to a job I never enjoyed. I spent hours leading up to each drive thinking about how gruesome the traffic would be. I spent five hours driving each day, which did not include my drive to other places outside of work. While my salary was generous, I could never justify the long commute. You may think there is an amount of money that will keep you commuting a dangerous number of hours, but I promise you, there is no amount of money worth your quality of life. Always ask yourself if the commute is worth it. If you come to discover the cost is not worth the ask, know another more suitable offer will come.

Is the Salary Worth the Work?

Certain companies are sneaky with their job descriptions. They will pay you the average amount for your position, but you end up doing work above your pay grade. Review the job description *thoroughly* and ask questions during your interview to fully know the expectations. If there is a statement that says, "Other duties outside of this job description may be performed," make sure you are comfortable with the salary they are offering. Chances are, you *will* be doing work that is out of scope.

Do They Match Your 401(k) Contributions?

I believe we—Millennials and Generation Z—may never see a single social security check in our lifetime. By the time we are old enough to qualify, it won't exist. What *will* exist is your 401(k), which you should always contribute to, whether or not your company matches. While this is rare at larger organizations, if the company making you an offer does not match your 401(k) contributions, you need to consider that. As I have mentioned, a 401(k) match is additional money on top of your base salary. Understand that for every company that does not match, there are five more that will.

What Is the Company Culture?

You can kid yourself all day long if you believe you can work for a company that goes against everything you stand for. I have left jobs and turned down tens of offers simply because the company culture was not for me. *Do not* simply accept an offer or remain with a company for the money. Full-time employees work an average of 2,080 hours each year. That is two thousand hours of your life you spend engaging with colleagues, vendors, and leadership. Working for a company with a poor culture can be detrimental to your mental health, further decreasing your quality of work. Money cannot fix a toxic work environment brought on by a cultural mismatch.

What Kind of Insurance Plans Are Offered?

It is important to analyze the insurance plans companies offer, and it is even more important to know what percentage they are willing to cover. Some employers will cover 70 percent of the cost, resulting in you paying for the rest. This is the bi-monthly insurance amount they deduct from each paycheck. Some organizations will cover 100 percent of your costs if you are single. These types of deductions are things you should consider when looking at job offers. A higher salary by a few thousand dollars doesn't mean much if you are paying for 30 percent of your health insurance costs.

Are There Career Advancement Opportunities?

Discussing career advancement opportunities with current *employees* is the only way to ensure what the employer is saying is true. Some companies may insinuate that career advancement is available, yet you join and remain in the same role for five years. Career advancement can lead to a higher salary and more benefits. So, while an offer you have at the moment is promising more money than you've ever seen before, think about where you can go after achieving your goals in that role. Can you move up and grow within the organization? Is there opportunity for exposure to other areas? All these questions are important to consider in your decision-making process.

Don't feel you have to accept every job offer that comes your way. Companies pass up amazing candidates all the time. You can pass up a company too, no matter your reasoning. Beyond building your network and yourself, a general blueprint applies to all career fields. To grow as a professional, you must commit to Step 1: Elevation, Step 2: Stabilization, and Step 3: Transition.

Step 1: Elevation

Elevation doesn't always mean moving into the next job title. If you reach the managerial level and decide the responsibility of a directorship isn't for you, there are other ways to elevate your career. Going back to school to get your master's, doctorate, or certification are a few ways to elevate, as they often bring on raises and other opportunities. Working to acquire advanced degrees keeps you agile in your career field, which people who desire to always keep learning appreciate. Many people reach a place of complacency and wonder why aspects of their careers have not changed for the better. They didn't do what was necessary for that growth to occur. These people remain in a role for too long without a raise, bonus, or any career development guidance. Keep in mind that elevation can mean *elevating* out of a company for a lateral or vertical shift. If your company isn't investing in you, *leave*. If you feel you are managing yourself, *leave*. Finally, if you feel there are benefits at another organization that make you happier regarding your career development, *leave*. Without elevation, you are unable to conquer your career in the way a true Career Savage would.

Step 2: Stabilization

Stabilization is when you nurture your elevation or *growth* for weeks, months, or even a few years. This is where your experience is gained for Step 3. During this stage, you are hyper-focused on becoming an invaluable subject matter expert. People often wonder how you know the stabilization stage has run its course. It's a cliché, but you truly will know when you are ready to move on. In some cases, you know you are ready, but fear manages to block moving onto the next step. In moments of fear, remember, growth is impossible without necessary change.

Step 3: Transition

Transitioning is the most exciting step. This is the graduation stage of career development. You are ready to take on your next role, business venture, or accept your advanced degree from your institution. A transition is brief as you are preparing to step back onto the stage of elevation. This is the stage where you are searching for opportunities or planning your next move.

These three steps are also applicable in entrepreneurship and personal development. You should always work to advance yourself and your business. If you are in a stage of exploration, choose one area to invest your time and see the other three steps through. If you find yourself displeased with your first chosen area, choose a new area and begin the cycle again. When I started Career Savage, my logos, website, and entire content plan were different from what they are today, and I can assure you they may change again. When I first started this brand, I elevated into entrepreneurship. There have been moments of stability followed by a transition and, yet again, another moment of elevation.

I've always known that climbing the corporate ladder as a twenty-something would be a challenge. I didn't know how unbelievably savvy I needed to be to avoid being taken advantage of and undervalued. Older generations have this weird mentality that makes them believe a twenty-something with a few years of experience is no match for their thirty years in the industry. Sometimes, this is true, but it's not always a fact. I have trained older persons, from medical doctors to industry veterans whose years of experience are greater than my age. The number of years doesn't directly correlate with the knowledge a person has. Previous colleagues of mine have had ten to twenty years of experience working at the same job, whereas my experience was diversified. As you elevate, stabilize, and transition into new opportunities, people will tell you how your few years don't support the years required to succeed in the role. Don't listen to this poor advice. It's *never* going to be about how many years you did something but rather what you did while there.

CHAPTER 9

A Savage Life

"Success is what you deem it to be. Always follow
your own definition, not society's."

—KYYAH ABDUL

For years, I thought success equated to a medical degree. I always
imagined working directly with patients, yelling "stat" across
the emergency room floor like all the residents on every medical
drama TV series. I thought I would own a private practice and
be known for my extensive clinical research and innovative
practices. Clearly, none of this happened, and while it could
still be my reality during my third or fourth decade of life, I
would only be chasing an archaic view of success. At a certain
point, I stopped chasing my parents' definition of success and
decided to pursue my own. Success is a weird concept because
it's subjective. For some people in their mid-twenties, success is
finally understanding what they want to do with their life and
working toward that goal. For others, it could be gaining total
independence. There is no objective definition of success, no
matter what anyone tells you. Society allows us to believe that
monetary wealth means you are successful. If you can afford a
Chanel bag, a Bentley, or a lavish vacation, you've made it in life.

A large percentage of people, apart from celebrities and the 1 percent, stretch beyond their means to afford this type of lifestyle. You see it every day on Instagram and TikTok. So how can this be classified as success when the portrayal of that very "success" is nothing more than a ruse? And what good is monetary wealth if you live in sadness? We have seen countless beloved celebrities cry out in misery despite having everything at their disposal. It is irrefutable to the percentage of millionaires/billionaires who are among some of the unhappiest people in the world. Don't get me wrong; money does provide a comfortable lifestyle, but it isn't everything. The point I am trying to make is that success is what you deem it to be! Always follow your definition, not society's.

Growing up in a Nigerian household, my parents ingrained *doctor* into my brain. They believed that becoming a doctor was a major key to being successful in America, with the bonus of having indisputable bragging rights within the Nigerian community. I can't fault my parents for believing this fallacy. They only knew so much about American opportunities. As Nigerian immigrants, they listened to the testimonies of immigrants who came before them. "Go to America and become a doctor, lawyer, or engineer to ensure you are never out of work. You can work anywhere in the world," they heard.

While it is true that the world needs these three occupations to function, these careers are not the only ones that provide job security. They also aren't the only jobs that allow you to work anywhere in the world.

The COVID-19 pandemic taught us that productivity isn't mutually exclusive with an office space. Throughout the years, I have talked my mother through gainful medical opportunities that do not require a medical degree. With each conversation, she became less rigid. My mother went from guilting me by saying, "Your father would have been so proud to see one of his children become a doctor," to the most supportive and understanding parent. She let go of her dream for me and began to let me live out my own. My life is my own, like how your life is your own. You can't allow your family or friends to back you into a career corner, forcing you to believe the career path they advise is the best and only option—the only road to success. The biggest key to living a successful and savage life is fulfilling your passions with grit, resilience, and ambition.

Luck of the Draw

I consider myself lucky. Following my parents' guidance early, I studied science and graduated with my degree in biology. I worked for hospitals, retail healthcare centers, clinics, and pharmaceutical corporations. I have researched rare diseases, studied diseases that disproportionately affect diverse populations, moderated patient focus groups, and I have loved every moment spent doing each one of these tasks. I know this isn't the case for everyone. I could have easily gone to school and graduated only to realize I didn't care for science. Some of you started college loving your major and, over the years, have grown to dislike your field of study. Some of you may change your major and some may graduate with a degree you know you never plan to use. Whatever you plan to do, know you can still live a successful and savage life regardless of what your diploma says.

The difference between entering college misguided and loving what you do as a college graduate can sometimes be a matter of luck. Don't let my luck and the luck of others trick you into believing you have to remain in the field you chose when you were eighteen. Some students graduate with a degree in communications, enter the workforce, and later decide to pursue a career in clinical research. Some students go to school for biology and graduate with a degree in something completely different such as art history, because they decided to switch their major sophomore year. The path you chose at eighteen does not have to be the path you remain on for the rest of your life. You may change your mind and want to try something else. You may get a job after college, work, and decide you want to travel for three months instead. You may want to start your own business completely unrelated to what you went to school for. You may decide that YouTube and social media influencing is what you were put on this earth to do. All of these options are okay. Everyone has different career ideas they want to attempt, and you should be no different.

The Savage Balance

When I first graduated, all I cared about was making money because, well, I was broke. I hated working in a pharmacy, but I knew I needed to keep that job to support myself. I've always thought that no matter what I desire to pursue, I must work to maintain my lifestyle. I didn't have the privilege of financially depending on my parents so I set a firm rule as I embarked on my career journey. As a new graduate, you may get into the workforce and detest everything about it: unfriendly coworkers, the rat race of a nine-to-five, and the unbearable commute. Despite this, remain in the workforce and climb your industry's hierarchy until you can financially support yourself while pursuing your other ventures full-time.

I have been working on Career Savage since 2017. Because it can't solely support my lifestyle and I like what I do, I keep working at my day job while strengthening the foundation of my business. Many social media influencers are college graduates; some even have their master's and doctoral degrees. Many of them have revealed the number of years it took before they could quit their jobs to become full-time influencers. This is the case for most of your favorites on social media. They pursued their passions while nurturing their security blankets. If influencing didn't work out, they had a career to fall back on. For some, success within their passion comes sooner than expected. Look at Megan thee Stallion and Saweetie. Both went to college and before ever needing to think of applying their degrees, their musical careers took off. Megan is truly an exceptional case. Her musical success soared beyond expectations while she was still in school. She worked on final essays while traveling to her sold-out shows.

This entire phenomenon of pursuing two things at once, one for financial stability and the other for fulfillment, is what I call the "Savage Balance." You simultaneously work toward two career goals until one surpasses the other. Some young people may see this as toxic, overworking yourself only to feed into the world of capitalism. I disagree. I work hard now so I won't have to work as hard later. My savage balance has resulted in a growing platform geared toward helping others advance on a professional level while evolving as a research and development professional. Even if I don't see myself remaining in research and development forever, I will still ensure I devote myself to evolving in that industry until I no longer want or need to. From associate to associate director, let my story be an example of what your story can be.

By now, you understand what savage balance is and how you can either be a Career Savage with savage balance or simply focus on one career development goal at a time. Both are acceptable, but what's more important to understand than anything you've read here is why you choose to do what you do. Understand your *why*. Being a young Nigerian American woman in corporate America comes with extreme challenges. You are muted, ridiculed, and assumed to hold a lesser title than you do. It's a cliché, but I work in clinical research because I desire to be the change I want to see. I have held certain job titles, but the one I desire most is the title that commands the most attention: a C-suite title. I have only ever seen one woman of color in the C-suite of a clinical research organization or pharmaceutical company. Often, pharmaceutical and medical decisions made for the minority community happen in the absence of representation. Diverse communities will continue to be wary of clinical research and the healthcare industry should both continue to lack diversity in leadership. I choose to continue to navigate the corporate pharmaceutical industry for these reasons. I created Career Savage to help other students navigate their careers with purpose. I choose to make the platform's continual growth a top priority to ensure more students are well equipped with career knowledge while in college and after. My "why" isn't rooted in money or fulfilling the career objectives others think I should. My "why" is rooted in a deeper purpose.

I've said it before—money isn't everything, and it shouldn't be why you choose to pursue your career. Sometimes your pursuit of money is the very thing that prevents you from enjoying your work. Money will come when you work hard, so there is no need to chase it. Yes, we need money to survive. Earlier I stated that when I first graduated, I only cared about making money because

I didn't have any, but overall, by the time I graduated college, my career ambitions were not rooted in capital gain.

Take a moment to think of your why. Your why is your target. Aiming in your career will be that much easier when you know what you are targeting.

What's My "Why"?

Starting a Business

My savage balance included the Career Savage franchise. I never knew I would start my own business, but when I did, I was elated to begin. Starting a business requires a lot of persistence. In the beginning, there will be weeks your business does well and other weeks where it doesn't. Don't be discouraged.

If the idea of starting your own business as a side opportunity resonates with you, understand that nowadays, you don't need a business plan to begin unless you plan on applying for loans or seeking investors. All you need to do is start and figure out the logistics while running your business.

Start-Up Business Tips	
Website	GoDaddy or Wix: GoDaddy is cheaper, but Wix has more to offer. Wix gives you a variety of options when building your website, while GoDaddy is more basic. With Wix, you can also embed an online store and take payments. Both offer domain purchasing, and they are not extensively different in terms of pricing. There are other options outside of GoDaddy and Wix, so do your research. Approximate annual fee: $300 *Prices may vary*
LLC Filing	Legal Zoom: Registering your business is pricey, so make sure you can afford to foot the bill before filing. Legal Zoom will attempt to convince you to make them your registered agent, but don't allow it. You can be your own registered agent and save $159 per year. There are certain legalities associated with being your own registered agent so make sure you know what you're getting yourself into. An LLC essentially protects you, personally, from getting sued. If you think filing an LLC is necessary, do some research as there are other options outside Legal Zoom. Approximate one-time fee: $250 Statement of Infor mation fee: $25 Taxing fee: $800 annual minimum *Prices may vary*
Business Cards	Vista Print or Moo: Vista Print is far more cost-efficient, but Moo is better quality. Approximate one-time fee: $25–$60 for 100 cards *Prices may vary*

Social Media Accounts	Make sure your business is on every social media platform possible (e.g., Instagram, TikTok, Facebook, Twitter, Pinterest, LinkedIn). If you don't want your employer to know about your business, follow my social media account separation steps in Chapter 3.
Business Email Accounts	When you build your website on any of the platforms mentioned above, there will be an offer to create a business email account. Of course, this is an extra monthly cost. If need be, use a free email account until you can pay for a business account monthly. Approximately $5 to $10 a month for a single account *Prices may vary*
Business Checking Accounts	Banks always offer promotions for opening a business account (e.g., $300 after depositing $1,500 of new money). Check with banks in your area to see what offers they have for new business accounts. Having a business account legitimizes your business. Sure, you can accept Venmo, QuickPay, and CashApp and mix your business and personal money, but this is not advised. The business account will make it easier to track your income. When it comes time to file your taxes, things will become more seamless.
Business Credit Card	Banks also offer promotions for opening a business credit card. Only opt to get a business credit card if it makes absolute sense. If you struggle with managing your money or the credit cards you already have, get comfortable first and then consider getting a business credit card.

When you first start, you may not even require all that is listed above. A good start would be social media accounts and a website. As your business grows, you can add other components.

When you are thinking of starting a business, ensure you are the solution to a problem. Solution-based businesses often see more success. Tesla solves the issue of gas cars degrading the environment. Instacart solves the issue of people being too busy to complete household tasks. Task Rabbit, Lyft, LinkedIn, Class Pass, and several other businesses are all solution-based. While the idea of starting a business seems cool, truly think about why you are doing it and if you can devote the appropriate amount of time to maintaining it. Do you need extra capital from the business to do something else? Do you enjoy the work of your business? I often see businesses fail because there is no mission and no solution to an actual problem. Take a moment to write out goals and objectives for your business.

I suggest writing in pencil or copying this table into another notebook as your goals and objectives may evolve over time.

Goals and Objectives

Mission

What problem
am I solving?

How am I solving it?

Target demographic

Marketing plan

Budget

Three-month goal

Six-month goal

One-year goal

Dream Even Bigger

You will learn that when you have big dreams, your dreams will force you to outgrow certain relationships. Certain people around you will attempt to squander your dreams, make you doubt yourself, and make you feel it's not possible or that pursuing your idea is irrelevant because it already exists. There are hundreds of bloggers and YouTubers making great money doing what they love, all in the same area of expertise. Do you know how many pages I come across on Instagram and TikTok that have "MUA" or "Food blogger" in their biography? There are hundreds of boutique coffee shops and hundreds of restaurants. There will always be someone trying to do what you want to do, but that does not mean you should not attempt to achieve your dreams. Don't let friends with self-limiting beliefs or skeptical family members keep you from getting your business started. Make your dreams come true by believing in yourself and putting forth the actions to achieve the unimaginable.

During my gap year, after college, I decided I needed to leave New Haven. The environment I was in made me feel like I was trapped in a bubble of complacency. I would go to sleep and wake up in a deep sweat after dreaming of a future I never wanted. Wake up, go to work, come home, and repeat. Staying in the same job for forty years followed by retirement was not the life I ever envisioned for myself, yet I was on a steady path to getting there. I decided leaving New Haven to pursue my master's would be the best option to getting the life I wanted. Amid completing the application process, gaining acceptance, and preparing to move, I began mobilizing Career Savage. There was no name, website, Instagram account, nothing. It was merely a few ideas jotted down in a notebook, everything from concepts to potential mission statements. My house in Connecticut was empty, my car was shipped back to my family residence in California, and I quit my job. All that was left to do was wait for my one-way flight from EWR to LAX in a few days. I sat in the basement of my then boyfriend's two-story family home in New Jersey, researching color psychology and exploring potential names for the business. After hours of brainstorming, I decided on "Career Savage." When he returned home from work, I presented my logo and ideas with enthusiasm. I was high on creativity and ambition.

He took no more than a five-second glance at my presentation and blurted out, "It'll never work. Do you even have a business plan?"

I turned my laptop around and said, "No, and I don't need one to get started. I am not starting a company that requires external capital."

He smugly said, "Yeah, okay. We will see how that works out for you." At that moment, I couldn't believe the lack of support I was receiving from someone I was so close to. Four days went by, he dropped me off at EWR, and we never spoke again.

Career Savage was my vision, and only I could understand how it would come to fruition. Some people told me to keep my head down and stay focused on my science career, but I always knew I could do both if I worked hard enough. The same goes for you if you choose to start a business or choose an unexpected path. Your family, boyfriend/girlfriend, or close friends may not understand why you choose to nurture your ideas. People won't always understand your ideas, and that's why they are *your* ideas. Pushing past communal doubt can make it challenging to stay motivated, but there are ways. When faced with everything but support, here are ten Career Savage motivational steps to fall back on:

1. Continually check in on your ever-evolving "Why": Sometimes we think the "what" and "how" are all that matter, but the number one way to stay motivated while pursuing what you want out of life is to stay connected to your "why"—the purpose behind what you are doing. Always remember that your "why" can evolve as you do.

2. Set realistic goals: Setting the goal to have your business up and running in one week or the goal to successfully transition into a new career and love every aspect of it overnight is wildly unrealistic. When you set unrealistic goals and don't meet them, you allow yourself to believe working toward your goals results in zero success. This may result in you slowly giving up. Rather than saying you will have your business up and running in one week, try to set multiple mini-goals and complete those. First, see step three for more guidance.

3. Complete one step of one goal at a time: You may overwhelm yourself when you have a few massive goals. It is better to have smaller goals you can work toward. For example, many of you may be living at home on the brink of losing your mind and wishing you were back in your college apartment far away from nagging parents. Rather than saying, "I'm going to move out tomorrow" with zero money saved up, it may be better to have goals leading up to your goal of moving out: (1a) Save up three months' worth of rent, security deposit, and money for household items; (1b) Work on credit score for apartment applications; (1c) Make a list of things you are looking for in an apartment; (1d) Set a budget for living alone; (1e) Browse and purchase household items in increments. Notice how each goal creates an opportunity for

achievement? Sometimes the little achievements provide the most motivation.

4. Remain positive: To remain positive while in an unmotivated state, it is best to practice gratitude. Think of how far you have come. What you have accomplished thus far. Refrain from comparing yourself to other people, but surround yourself with inspirational people. This brings me to my next piece of advice.

5. Surround yourself with like-minded people: Everyone knows the saying, "misery loves company." Well, the same saying applies to career advancement. If you are surrounded by complacent people, you are more likely to experience a lack of motivation. Take the example of my unsupportive partner. His lack of faith in me stemmed from his mindset, which was stagnant at the time. He merely projected his state of mind onto my career plans. When you surround yourself with like-minded people, they inspire and often motivate you to achieve whatever you find desirable.

6. Visualize your goals on hard and easy days: When I attended track meets in high school, I felt apprehensive about my upcoming races. I feared losing so greatly that my coaches would pull me from races. They were concerned for me and my anxiety. To combat this fear, I began to visualize winning each race. To my surprise, it always worked. Whether I came in third, second, or first place, I was motivated to try my best. Imagining your end goal can serve as a great motivator. If you are struggling to find some motivation, think about why you are working as hard

as you are. Think about how relieved you will feel after reaching that goal.

7. Modify your environment to improve your mood: Environment can easily contribute to a lack of motivation. Amid the COVID-19 pandemic, we still saw many people losing motivation to work and even be creative. For almost one year and counting, people are occasionally prohibited from leaving their homes or entering facilities that provide grounds for social interaction. We worked, laughed, vacationed, ate four meals, and slept in our houses for nearly one year straight. Some of us are still having to remain within our homes as the pandemic continues with the rise of new variants. After a while, you grow tired of seeing the same four walls. The COVID-19 global pandemic has proven the importance of modifying your environment to spark inspiration and motivation.

8. Everything doesn't have to be serious: A lack of motivation can stem from an absence of fun. Achieving your goals doesn't mean you can't enjoy yourself while doing so. When I lost motivation to create YouTube content for Career Savage, I introduced new concepts such as Wine Down Wednesday and interviews with people from different professions. Every video didn't have to be me talking into the camera. Ever since I began working on these new initiates, my motivation to create content has remained consistent. Should I experience another wave, I will develop new and fun ways to make my goal of creating Career Savage content.

9. Starve your distractions: Social media used to be one of my biggest distractions. I would spend hours comparing myself to others. The comparison resulted in me adding additional unnecessary goals because I saw others checking them off their list. For example, I saw a career coach successfully expanding her business on Pinterest. Just because she was doing it did not mean I needed to work toward that. Since this realization, I've let the idea of expanding on Pinterest go. The path that this career coach took doesn't mean it's the path I'm meant to take. After taking six months off from all social media, I realized I needed to develop a healthier relationship with it. I now spend no more than one hour daily on all social media platforms. Most of my usage comes from my daily posts and stories on Instagram. I have also learned to see every post, comment, and DM as 0.1 percent of the truth. If social media is not the distraction that needs starving, simply apply the same practice to whatever is holding you back.

10. Reward yourself: Whatever you enjoy, reward yourself with it as you accomplish steps toward reaching your end goal. Sometimes your reward can simply be a weekend off from feeding your ambition, or it can be a material gift to yourself for reaching an important milestone.

Career Savages Aren't Born, They're Made

A *savage* life is what you deem it to be. As I mentioned at the start of this chapter, success is subjective. In building your savage life, success becomes the byproduct. This can only mean that a savage life is also subject to the opinion of each person. One person may feel a savage life gives them the ability to buy anything they want without looking at the price tag or being creative every day and not caring how much money someone else is making. You've made it to the end of this guide. I am sure a million things, from motivation to uncertainty, are running through your mind. Whichever it is, you should feel accomplished in seeking this knowledge. From the summer before senior year to the years that follow, you can evolve into the professional, entrepreneur, or creative you want to be by following the overarching steps you've read.

In Chapter 2, you learned how to get an internship before starting your senior year, and you learned the importance of internships for navigating your career field. In Chapter 3, senior year began, and you continued to apply what you learned in the summer throughout your first semester while resisting the temptation to engage in every *last* college event. In Chapter 4, you learned that sacrifices are sometimes necessary for success, and experience should continue to be gained even during winter vacation. In Chapter 5, you learned second-semester senioritis could pull you back from reaching your goals, and you learned ways to remedy the symptoms. In Chapter 6, you learned spring break is fun, but having a job after graduation is even better. In Chapter 7, you learned the importance of taking time to appreciate your education and the opportunities that will come as a result. You also learned reflection is an integral part of being successful. In Chapter 8, you picked up tools for achieving and maintaining success as a postgraduate. You learned about everything from job offers to remote working tips. Finally, in Chapter 9, you learned the steps you can take to kickstarting entrepreneurship and believing in the vision you have for yourself. More importantly, you learned your life, career, and successes are what *you* decide them to be.

As you embark further along your career journey, take with you all that you have learned. Be patient and optimistic that you will find your way the more you expose yourself to. Accept that growth is a part of success, and you can't reach higher heights without it. A *career savage* is no longer who you will become but rather who you are. Congratulations on finishing the first step.

Afterword

I want to personally thank you for taking the time to read my first-ever book. I hope you enjoyed reading it as much as I enjoyed writing it. My life experiences are told as a way for you to feel connected to me and a way for you to understand where my advice derives from. I want to hear about your experiences before and after reading this book. I would like to invite you to find me on Instagram (@KyyahAbdul and @CareerSavage) and send me a message whenever you feel inclined. I try to answer all my messages and rarely miss the opportunity to engage with others.

I always welcome feedback as I feel it's important for growth. Please let me know what you think about this book by emailing me at info@careersavage.com, leaving a comment on a *Career Savage* YouTube video (www.youtube.com/c/careersavage) or leaving a review of the book on Amazon. I hope to keep providing readers and viewers with career guidance, and I hope you come back to hear more from me.

Again, thank you for reading!

With kindness,

About the Author

Kyyah Abdul is the founder of *Career Savage*, a platform curated to address issues within the college education system by providing college students and working professionals with present-day career advice.

Before writing *The Prepared Graduate*, Kyyah served as a resident blogger for *The Iconic Girls*. She has cowritten public health programs addressing ways to decrease the prevalence of poor cardiovascular health among the African American population and is a published coauthor on a scientific article.

She holds a BS in pre-medical biology from the University of New Haven and an MPH concentrated in urban healthcare disparities from Charles R. Drew University of Medicine and Science. As a public health and regulatory affairs professional, Kyyah works with health authorities to get quality medicines to the public quicker while also advocating for the representation of marginalized communities in clinical research settings.

Kyyah Abdul was raised in Palos Verdes, California, a suburban peninsula within Los Angeles County. She prides herself on being a Nigerian American Africanist and appreciates the richness of her culture. When she is not advising, writing, or working in clinical research, Kyyah spends most of her time traveling solo or with friends and family. She believes the greatest treasure in life comes from the memories made with loved ones.

Kyyah hopes you read this book and feel more than **prepared** to take on anything life has in store for you.

Keep in touch with Kyyah via the web:

Websites:
www.careersavage.com
www.kyyahabdul.com

YouTube:
www.Youtube.com/c/careersavage &
www.YouTube.com/c/KyyahAbdul

Instagram:
www.instagram.com/kyyahabdul/

TikTok:
www.tiktok.com/@kyyahabdul

Twitter:
www.twitter.com/KyyahAbdul

References

1. Hanson, Melanie. "Education Data." College Graduation Statistics. Last modified August 9, 2021. https://educationdata.org/number-of-college-graduates.

2. Snyder, Thomas D. (ed.). *120 Years of American Education: A Statistical Portrait*. US Department of Education Office of Educational Research and Improvement. January 1993. https://nces.ed.gov/pubs93/93442.pdf.

3. US Bureau of Labor Statistics. "Establishment Age and Survival Data." Last modified July 28, 2021. www.bls.gov/bdm/bdmage.htm.

4. Harvard University. "Harvard University History." Last modified 2021. https://www.harvard.edu/about-harvard/harvard-history/.

5. Best College Reviews Staff Writers. "The History Behind Harvard University." April 27, 2021. https://www.bestcollegereviews.org/history-behind-harvard-university.

6. The University of Virginia. "About the University." Last modified 2021. www.virginia.edu/aboutuva.

7. Act of July 2, 1862 (Morrill Act), Public Law 37-108, which established land grant colleges, 07/02/1862; Enrolled Acts and Resolutions of Congress, 1789-1996; Record Group 11; General Records of the United States Government; National Archives.

8. US Department of Veterans Affairs. "History and Timeline." Education and Training. Last modified November 21, 2013. https://www.benefits.va.gov/gibill/history.asp.

9. National Center for Education Statistics. "Degrees conferred by postsecondary institutions, by level of degree and sex of student: Selected years, 1869–70 through 2029–30." Table prepared July 2020. https://nces.ed.gov/Programs/Digest/D20/Tables/Dt20_318.10.Asp.

10. Cornell University. "Workbook: Facts about Cornell Public." Published 2021. https://tableau.cornell.edu/t/IRP/views/FactsaboutCornellPublic/QuickFactsaboutCornell?:embed=y&:loadOrderID=0&:display_spinner=no&:display_count=no&:showVizHome=no.

11. Bergman, Dave. "Acceptance Rates at Ivy League & Elite Colleges—Class of 2025." College Transitions. April 9, 2021. https://www.collegetransitions.com/blog/ivy-league-acceptance-rates-class-of-2025/.

12. Machovich, Ron. "More than 8,800 offered fall admission to USC, from historically large pool of applicants." USC News. March 30, 2021. https://news.usc.edu/183939/usc-2021-admissions-first-generation-students/.

13. Carnevale, Anthony P., Nicole Smith, and Jeff Strohl. *Recovery: Job Growth and Education Requirements Through 2020—Executive Summary.* Georgetown Public Policy Institute. June 10, 2013. https://cew.georgetown.edu/wp-content/uploads/2014/11/Recovery2020.ES_.Web_.pdf.

14. Association of American Colleges & Universities. "Employers Agree: College Degrees are Worth It?". AAC&U News. September 2018. https://www.aacu.org/aacu-news/newsletter/2018/september/facts-figures.

15. Borden, Taylor, and Dominic-Madori Davis. "How much money you need to make to live comfortably in every state in America?" *Business Insider.* Last modified March 10, 2021.

https://www.businessinsider.com/personal-finance/living-wage-income-to-live-comfortably-in-every-us-state?.

16. Statista. "Median household income in the United States in 2019, by educational attainment of householder." September 2020. https://www.statista.com/statistics/233301/median-household-income-in-the-united-states-by-education/.

17. Semega, Jessica, Melissa Kollar, Emily A. Shrider, and John F. Creamer. *Income and Poverty in the United States: 2019*. United States Census Bureau. Last modified September 2021. https://www.census.gov/content/dam/Census/library/publications/2020/demo/p60-270.pdf.

18. Oyer, Paul. "Initial Labor Market Conditions and Long-Term Outcomes for Economists." *Journal of Economic Perspectives* 20, no. 3 (Summer 2006): 143–160. https://doi.org/10.1257/jep.20.3.143.

19. Center on Budget and Policy Priorities. "Chart Book: The Legacy of the Great Recession." June 6, 2019. https://www.cbpp.org/research/economy/the-legacy-of-the-great-recession.

20. US Bureau of Labor Statistics. (2012, February). *BLS Spotlight on Statistics: The Recession of 2007–2009*. Published 2012. https://www.bls.gov/spotlight/2012/recession/pdf/recession_bls_spotlight.pdf.

21. Falk, Gene, Paul D. Romero, Isaac A. Nicchitta, and Emma C. Nyhof. *Unemployment Rates During the COVID-19 Pandemic*. Congressional Research Service. Last modified August 20, 2021. https://sgp.fas.org/crs/misc/R46554.pdf.

22. US Census Bureau. "Income, Poverty and Health Insurance Coverage in the US: 2020." Last modified October 8, 2021. https://www.census.gov/newsroom/press-releases/2021/income-poverty-health-insurance-coverage.html.

Mango Publishing, established in 2014, publishes an eclectic list of books by diverse authors—both new and established voices—on topics ranging from business, personal growth, women's empowerment, LGBTQ studies, health, and spirituality to history, popular culture, time management, decluttering, lifestyle, mental wellness, aging, and sustainable living. We were recently named 2019 *and* 2020's #1 fastest-growing independent publisher *Publishers Weekly*. Our success is driven by our main goal, which is to publish high-quality books that will entertain readers as well as make a positive difference in their lives.

Our readers are our most important resource; we value your input, suggestions, and ideas. We'd love to hear from you—after all, we are publishing books for you!

Please stay in touch with us and follow us at:
    Facebook: Mango Publishing
    Twitter: @MangoPublishing
    Instagram: @MangoPublishing
    LinkedIn: Mango Publishing
    Pinterest: Mango Publishing
    Newsletter: mangopublishinggroup.com/newsletter

Join us on Mango's journey to reinvent publishing, one book at a time.

CPSIA information can be obtained
at www.ICGtesting.com
Printed in the USA
JSHW030208230222
23249JS00006B/126